ACCOUNTING FOR NON FINANCIAL MANAGERS

ACCOUNTING
FOR
NON
FINANCIAL
MANAGERS

MERWIN LEVEN

BOARDROOM® BOOKS
500 Fifth Avenue, New York, New York 10110

$50

The author expresses deep appreciation to John W. Seder
for assistance in the preparation of this manuscript.

Library of Congress Cataloging in Publication Data

Leven, Merwin.
    Accounting for nonfinancial managers.

    Includes index.
    1. Accounting.   I. Title.
HF 5635.L64   657   80-19502
ISBN 0-932-648-16-9

Second Printing

TABLE OF CONTENTS

Chapter One

ACCOUNTING:
THE LANGUAGE OF FINANCE

Accounting is a language for expressing financial information. Like all language, accounting has rules and standards similar to grammar and syntax. And the key to successful communication in accounting, as in all languages, is uniform meaning of words. When the speaker (or writer) uses a particular word, both he and the listener (or reader) know exactly what it means. Complete agreement on the meaning of words is what changes a language from a jumble of symbols and sounds into an effective means of communication.

The words of accounting are, in many cases, unnecessarily obscure. Accountants, like all professionals, do much of their communicating in code or jargon. They use complex and unfamiliar terms to describe very ordinary things. In this book we shall try to translate the jargon of accounting into commonsense English.

Among the familiar words are the terms of the five basic building blocks of the accounting structure:

- Assets: what a business owns.

- Liabilities: what a business owes.

- Equity: the value of the ownership of the business (also called net worth).

- Expenses: the cost of purchases, wages and salaries, and other costs of running the business.

- Income: the money that comes into the business.

These are the five basic accounts that are used in keeping books of the business. Every number in the business that involves money will be recorded in at least one of these accounts, and many numbers go into two or three.

Reading and writing the language

Accountants and bookkeepers produce and use a great variety of forms, schedules, and reports. Some of these provide a wealth of detail about very small aspects of the business, while others summarize information and present totals that give an overview.

If a manager wants to get the fastest possible look at the overall financial picture of a business, he can do it by looking at three reports that present all of the important numbers in total form.

These three basic reports are:

- The balance sheet.

- The income statement or statement of income, sometimes also called the profit and loss statement.

- The statement of sources and uses of funds, sometimes called the statement of changes in financial position.

These statements can sometimes be condensed into only two pages of figures, although the explanatory notes may take several more pages. They report all of the basic information about the financial condition of the business on the date they were compiled and about the financial results of operations for the year (or other period of time) ending on that day.

Such reports give information in summary form--as totals--and it may sometimes be necessary to ask for a breakdown of the totals to get more detail. But it's all there. Everything the business owns and everything it owes is included somewhere in one of the three reports. And everything it does with money--all the money that came in and all the money that went out during the year--is included somewhere in all three reports, which form a closed loop, an integrated system. They are interconnected in many places and can be reconciled exactly with one another. If they can't be reconciled, then it will be clear that somebody has made a mistake and the accounts are not in order.

Chapter Two

THE BALANCE SHEET

The balance sheet of a corporation is like a snapshot of what the business owns, what it owes, and what the ownership is worth--in other words its assets, liabilities, and equity--as of an instant in time. It's not a movie but a still picture, and like a still picture of a busy city street where everybody is in motion, the picture will be out of date a moment after it is taken.

A balance sheet has three parts

Many people think that a balance sheet has two parts--assets on one side and liabilities on the other. That conception is not completely accurate. One side is assets, true enough. But the other side itself is divided into two parts: it consists of liabilities and equity, or net worth. That makes three parts altogether:

BALANCE SHEET OF ABC CORPORATION

Dec. 31,
1979

ASSETS

(what we own)

Dec. 31,
1979

LIABILITIES

(what we owe)

EQUITY

(net worth, or net ownership after

all bills are paid)

TOTAL   TOTAL

These totals will be exactly the same.

In examining the right side of the balance sheet, the so-called liability side, it's important to know where to draw that horizontal line that
separates liabilities (above the line) from equity (below the line). Experienced financial analysts are accustomed to drawing that line mental-
ly--it's one of the first things they do when they look at a balance sheet,
knowing its central function: it adds up what we own, then subtracts what we
owe. What's left is what we are worth, or equity. Many people are confused on
this fundamental point because they have heard so much about assets and
liabilities, instead of about assets, liabilities, and equity.

A personal balance sheet

Individuals can have balance sheets as well as corporations. In fact,
every individual has one, whether or not he knows it or has ever taken the

trouble to put it on paper. It may be helpful to look at an individual's balance sheet that is put together in the same way as the balance sheet of a corporation.

Here is a hypothetical balance sheet of an imaginary individual, a corporate executive in his forties who earns $75,000 a year and is married and has three children, one in college:

JOHN R. JONES

Balance Sheet

ASSETS	Feb. 1, 1980	LIABILITIES AND EQUITY	Feb. 1, 1980
Cash in checking account	$ 832	Credit card bills	$ 1,100
Passbook savings account	3,200	Tuition, room, and board payable for spring semester	3,700
Expense account reimbursement receivable	640	Mortgage payments due within one year	9,600
Six-month savings bank certificate	10,000		
TOTAL CURRENT ASSETS	$ 14,672	TOTAL CURRENT LIABILITIES	$ 14,400
Stocks	14,500	Home mortgage--amount due after one year	44,000
Municipal bonds	8,800		
Value of company stock option if exercised	22,000	Condominium mortgage-- amount due after one year	9,000
Four bedroom home, at cost	90,000		
Condominium in Stowe, Vt., at cost	21,000		
Automobiles, at market value	6,000		
Furniture and clothing, at fair market value	22,000	EQUITY	131,572
	$ 198,972		$ 198,972

Equity is a residual figure

This personal or family balance sheet is in three parts. The all-important third part appears on only one line, but note that it is the highest figure of all, except for the totals. This balance sheet adds up what the family owns, giving great emphasis to the most liquid and most current assets. Then it subtracts what the family owes, giving most prominence to the bills that must be paid first. Net worth or equity is what is left over. Thus, the equity figure is a residual figure: it is derived from the other totals on the balance sheet.

To put it another way, the equity figure is what makes the balance sheet balance. After adding up assets, and putting the total at the bottom on the left, we add up liabilities. Assuming the family or business is solvent, the total of liabilities is less than the total of assets. And this gap is filled by equity, and the total on the right side ends up the same as the total on the left.

A balance sheet emphasizes current assets
and liabilities

Note that this balance sheet is arranged so as to give special prominence to cash, and to assets that will soon be turned into cash--and to bills that have to be paid soon. Some of the other items on the balance sheet may be much larger--the house, for example--but the current items are listed first.

This makes sense, because a balance sheet is supposed to show financial condition; and the most important aspect of a family's (or company's) financial condition is the ability to pay its bills. If the family has a big house but no money to buy food, its current financial condition isn't very sound. We all know people like that, and there are many businesses in that situation too.

Thus the most prominent part of the balance sheet, the items at the top on the left, are current assets. That means cash and items that will be turned into cash in the ordinary course of events within a year or less. Other assets might be sold and turned into cash in a few days--stocks, for example--but it is not expected that they will be sold, and thus they are not considered current assets.

Current assets (and other assets too) are listed in the order of their convertibility into cash. Cash is always listed first, and the items that can be turned into cash most easily and rapidly are listed near the top. Each item is a bit harder to convert than the item above it and a bit easier than the item below it. Note that the last item on the list of assets is the family's used furniture and clothing.

Current liabilities are the bills that must be paid within a year or less, as distinguished from long-term liabilities that will be paid over a longer period. Note that the family's biggest debt obligations or liabilities, the mortgages, are divided into two parts. The payments due soon are included in current liabilities because they are the ones to worry about now.

Just as the assets are ranked in order of convertibility into cash, so the liabilities are ranked, with those at the top--credit card bills-- likely to be paid first.

Now let us look at an actual corporate balance sheet, which we will call that of the ABC Company:

The ABC Company

Balance Sheet
December 31, 1979

ASSETS			LIABILITIES	
Current Assets:			Current Liabilities:	
Cash		$ 9,353	Accounts Payable	$ 52,083
Marketable Securities (U.S. Treasury Bills)		27,649	Current Installment on Long-Term Debt	11,128
Accounts and Notes Receivable:			Accrued Expenses	35,172
Total	$109,023		Total Current Liabilities	98,383
Less: Allowance for	8,713	100,310		
Doubtful Accounts			Long-Term Debt	149,188
Inventories		76,013	Deferred Income Taxes	35,635
Prepaid Expenses		6,588	Total Liabilities	$283,206
Total Current Assets		$219,913	Commitments and Contingencies--See Notes to Balance Sheet	
Plant, Property,	$509,325		Shareholders' Equity:	
Less: Allowances for	224,289	285,036		
Depreciation and Depletion			Preferred Stock	2,727
			Common Stock	35,412
Investments		24,864	Capital Surplus	58,962
Other Assets		21,771	Retained Earnings	171,835
Total Assets		$551,584	Treasury Stock	(558)
			Total Shareholders' Equity	268,378
			Total Liabilities and Shareholders' Equity	$551,584

This corporate balance sheet, like the family balance sheet we looked at earlier, highlights the current assets and liabilities. And the three-part nature of the balance sheet is clearly shown, with the right side divided into two parts--liabilities and equity.

The equity part of the balance sheet

The most   item under shareholders equity is the total. But the preferred stock figure is important, too--listed first, since the preferred ranks ahead of the common stock, and its shareholders have a prior claim on the company's assets. The amount shown here is the total par value of all outstanding preferred stock.

The remaining items should be mentally lumped together to show the total book value of the common equity. The division among the three members is utterly without significance, except from a historical point of view. Here's how they developed: Many years ago the company sold shares having a par value or stated value of $5.00 per share at a price considerably higher than that. (Let's say it was $50.00). The first $5.00 received for each share was recorded in the common stock account and the rest in capital surplus. Thus, capital surplus is the amount invested by the original shareholders in excess of the par value of their shares.

Retained earnings is the total of profits (after taxes since the company started in business) that have been retained by the company and reinvested in the business rather than paid out as dividends.

"Treasury stock" is the amount paid by the company at various times in the past to buy or redeem its own stock. It is basically a nonsense figure, since stock in the treasury has no value or significance.

The significant number on this balance sheet is $265,651.* It is the book value of the common stock equity, which is the basic ownership of the company.

Certain other accounting rules and procedures that were used in preparing this balance sheet are not readily apparent from the figures.

Assets are not carried at current value but at cost

The general philosophy of accounting is to be as conservative as possible. One must at all costs avoid overstating the value of assets or income. It is not serious if they are understated; in fact, it is common. By the same token, liabilities and expenses must never be understated.

During an inflationary period, the value of everything we own tends to increase as the value of the dollar decreases. And the increase may be

*Total of common stock, capital surplus, and retained earnings, less treasury stock.

very large for land, buildings, and other properties that have been held for many years, as almost every homeowner knows. But it is a basic accounting principle that assets on the balance sheet are not marked up to reflect inflation or increases in the market value from other causes.

However, if asset values decrease for some reason, the value is adjusted accordingly. Thus the rule is that asset values are stated at depreciated* original cost, so long as that figure does not exceed current fair market value. If it does exceed market value, then the stated value must be reduced accordingly. As a result, the figure shown on the balance sheet will be either depreciated original cost or current fair market, whichever is lower. In accounting terminology, assets are carried at "lower of cost or market."

Look again at the personal balance sheet on page 7 and note that the house, which is worth more than it cost, is carried at cost. But the used furniture, clothing, and cars, which are worth less than they cost, have been marked down to market value.

Fixed asset values are reduced by depreciation

Assets are carried at cost, but it is an adjusted cost. The accountant puts the original cost on the balance sheet when the asset is acquired, but that figure is reduced every year by depreciation.

Suppose that on January 1, 1980 an auto parts manufacturing company buys a $100,000 metal stamping machine that it expects to use for 15 years. At the end of that time the manufacturer expects the machine to be worn out, and intends to sell it for scrap.

*We'll explain in the next section.

In this situation, it is a basic principle of accounting that the company would not consider the entire $100,000 as a business expense for the year 1980. To do so would give a misleading impression of the company's profits in 1980, or possibly even turn profits into losses. Since the company expects to use the machine for 15 years, it is not proper to treat the full cost as an expense in one year. Rather, the cost is spread over 15 years, with 1/15 of the cost ($6,667) being considered as an expense each year. This permits the cost of the machine to be charged to expense over its useful life.

Thus at the end of the first year, the machine would be carried on the balance sheet at $93,333, representing original cost ($100,000) less one year's depreciation. At the end of the second year it would be carried at $86,666, representing the $100,000 less two years' depreciation of $13,334 (2 x $6,667).

The stated value of the machine drops each year, and this is proper and reasonable, since the machine is undergoing wear and tear. Each year it is older and presumably less valuable.

Of course, some properties grow more valuable even as they grow older--for example, homes and office buildings--but the conventions of accounting require that they be depreciated, too. This fits with the conservative philosophy of accounting, which tries to avoid at all costs overstating the value of assets, but is not troubled if their value is understated.

The simplified example above used straight line depreciation. (There are other, more complicated depreciation methods, covered in more detail in Chapter 6.)

Assets carried at reduced values

Depreciation is only one example of the use of allowances to establish a reasonable value for assets that should not be carried at full value. Another example is the allowance for bad debts.

The ABC Company balance sheet shows that the company had customer accounts receivable totaling $109,023. Obviously it hoped to collect every dollar of that amount. But it has learned from experience that some customers will go bankrupt or refuse to pay. Realistically, it is likely to collect a bit less than the full amount shown.

Thus, the stated value of the receivables is reduced by the allowance for doubtful items and discounts, which is sometimes also known as a bad debt reserve. There are certain well-established accounting methods for determining the amount of the allowance. One approach is to write off (i.e., put into the allowance) a percentage of sales or a percentage of receivables; the percentage is determined by the company's bad debt experience in previous years. Another method is for management to review each customer's account and designate those accounts which it considers to be uncollectible.

The balance sheet carries only assets with identifiable costs

In line with the basic philosophy of conservatism, the balance sheet generally does not assign values to assets that cannot be appraised or evaluated with some degree of accuracy. A good example is trademarks and corporate goodwill. The names Chevrolet, Kodak, Ivory, and Hershey are obviously valuable--indeed, their owners have spent untold millions of dollars in advertising them and building their values. And if they were

14

offered for sale the prices might be in tens or even hundreds of millions of dollars.

But, say the accountants, since no costs are directly identifiable to these assets, they must either be eliminated from the balance sheet entirely or, if they are mentioned at all, they are assigned a nominal value. (Nominal means really nominal: General Motors' and Procter & Gamble's trademarks are carried at $1.00.)

What about liabilities that cannot be exactly identified? There may be some of those too; for example, a lawsuit pending against the company or obligations to pay future pensions, with no money yet put aside to cover the obligation. Since the amount cannot be calculated precisely, these liabilities are not carried on the balance sheet. However, the commitments and contingencies item is a cross-reference to an explanation of these items in the notes which accompany the balance sheet.

New balance sheet format emphasizing net working capital

We have seen that the balance sheet is usually presented in this form:

Current assets	$ xxx	Current liabilities	$ xxx
Fixed and other assets	xxx	Other liabilities	xxx
			$ x,xxx
		Equity	xxx
	$ x,xxx		$ x,xxx

A new and different format has been gaining favor in recent years. It presents the balance sheet figures in one column instead of two:

Current assets	$ xxx
Less: Current liabilities	xxx
NET WORKING CAPITAL	xxx
Plus: Fixed assets	x,xxx
Plus: Other assets	xxx
FUNDS EMPLOYED IN THE BUSINESS	$ x,xxx
Less: Long-term liabilities	xxx
EQUITY	$ x,xxx

This format highlights net working capital, which is the difference between current assets and current liabilities. Net working capital is considered to be one of the most important indicators of a company's financial condition, since it shows the relationship between cash and the items that will soon turn into cash, on one hand, and bills that will soon be paid on the other. Most financial analysts make a mental calculation of net working capital, and this format saves the trouble of doing that.

The corporate balance sheet presented earlier is shown in the new format in Appendix A on page 142.

Let us now summarize some balance sheet basics and also review what we can learn from the balance sheet. And also what it doesn't tell us.

1. A balance sheet is a snapshot. It shows how the company stands at an instant in time, often the close of business on December 31. By about 9:30 a.m. on January 2, the balance sheet will already be out of date. Bills may be paid, goods may be shipped, raw material may be received, contracts may be signed. The changes in the balance sheet figures may be small but there will certainly be changes within one day after the balance sheet is prepared. And, unless the company is very small, it will probably take at

16

least ten days to two weeks to gather all the figures and compile them into the balance sheet. As a result...

2. The balance sheet emphasizes liquidity. It gives great prominence to cash and "near cash"--those items that can be liquidated or turned into cash very easily and rapidly. Assets are listed on the balance sheet in order of liquidity.

3. One purpose of the balance sheet is to show the lender or creditor what the company has invested in the business. It does not show what its current value would be if the company were liquidated. The value of the business may be higher or lower than the balance sheet values, depending on the actual market value of the assets.

4. The balance sheet is out of date when you look at it. Most of the numbers will change during the time it takes to prepare the balance sheet. Thus, the information presented by the balance sheet could be very misleading. The reader must also ask whether any material transactions have taken place since the date of this balance sheet.

5. The balance sheet does not tell how the company is doing. The balance sheet may show (in retained earnings) that the company earned money in the past, but it doesn't tell you when. It is possible that the profits were earned many years ago, and that the company lost money last year and might lose more this year. That information must be found in the income statement (see page 28).

6. The balance sheet is very conservative. Assets may be understated but must never be overstated. Some asset values are reduced by amounts put into reserves. All assets are carried at adjusted cost or fair market value, whichever is lower. And the balance sheet does not recognize

inflationary increases in market values, even though these may be enormous. It is quite common, for example, to find that a factory, warehouse, or office building that was built many years ago has been written down (depreciated) to a fraction of its original cost. At the same time, its real market value has been increasing rather than decreasing. As a result, it may be worth 10 or 15 times as much as the figure stated on the balance sheet.

7. The balance sheet is in three parts--assets, liabilities, and equity. And equity is the residual figure--the amount of assets that would be left over if all the bills were paid. We have seen also that equity is a balancing figure. It is what makes the balance sheet balance so that the total of the left column (assets) exactly equals the right-hand total (liabilities and net worth).

Chapter Three

FUNDAMENTALS
OF BOOKKEEPING

A business' principal objective is to make a profit, and it accomplishes this by taking in more money than it spends. Thus, the movement of money and other valuable assets must be very tightly controlled and monitored.

The manager should thus insist that every transaction involving money and assets be carefully recorded under a bookkeeping system that is tight. There must be no escape hatches, no way for money to get lost or disappear.

The books must be kept in a precise and orderly manner, using the uniform language and conventions of accounting, so that each entry can be understood easily by the manager as well as the bookkeeper. And by strangers, too. If the books are kept properly, a visitor from Mars who understood accounting and bookkeeping could understand the books and accounts without a word of additional explanation. He would be able to tell where the money came from, where it went, how much is left, and where it is--

simply by examining the company's books.

The double entry system—debits and credits

Accountants and bookkeepers do a number of things to keep the system tight and avoid errors, but perhaps the most essential is the system of double entries. Every transaction is recorded twice. One of these entries is a debit and the other is a credit.

We have seen that the five basic accounts are assets, liabilities, equity, income, and expenses. A debit is an increase in assets, or expenses. A credit is an increase in liabilities, equity, or income. And a decrease in any item is the reverse.

Let us examine a number of ordinary transactions to see the two entries that are made for each one. Keep in mind that any movement of goods or money into or out of the company must be accounted for. (Note that increases on the left side of the balance sheet are debits, and increases on the right side are credits.)

(1) Company begins business. Owner invests $10,000 and issues stock to himself.

Debit (increase) cash $10,000. Credit (increase) common stock equity $10,000.

(2) Company borrows $5,000 from bank.

Debit (increase) cash $5,000. Credit (increase) loans payable (current liabilities) $5,000

(3) Company orders a machine for $12,000.

No entry, since no cash or assets have moved as yet.

(4) Machine is delivered.

Debit (increase) plant and equipment $12,000. Credit (increase) accounts payable $12,000.

(5) Company makes $5,000 part payment on machine.

Credit (decrease) cash $5,000. Debit (decrease) accounts payable $5,000.

(6) Company receives $2,000 worth of steel from supplier on credit.

Debit (increase) inventory $2,000.
Credit (increase) accounts payable $2,000.

(7) Company ships $1,000 worth of product to customer.

Credit (decrease) inventory $1,000.
Debit (increase) accounts receivable $1,000.

One easy way to visualize debits and credits is to use a "T" worksheet for each account. The T worksheet is not actually part of the books of account but is suggested as an aid in recording transactions.

CASH
1980
Feb. 1 (1) $10,000

Feb. 2 (2) $5,000

1980
Feb. 21
(5) $5,000

INVENTORY
Feb. 22 (6) $2,000

COMMON STOCK
1980
Feb. 1 (1) $10,000

LOANS PAYABLE
1980
Feb. 2 (2) $5,000

ACCOUNTS PAYABLE
1980
Feb. 21
(5) $5,000

Feb. 22 (6) $2,000

The bookkeeping routine

Since bookkeeping is a tightly controlled system, with no leaks or slippages, there is a systematic and orderly sequence of documents, with information transferred from one document to the next in this order:

- Original documents, or original evidence.

- Journal (book of original entry).

- Ledger.

- Trial balances.

- Adjusting entries.

• Working papers.

• Reports (balance sheet, income statement, statement of sources and uses of funds).

Original documents are bills, invoices, receipts, and other papers containing all of the detailed information about the transaction. For example, an invoice sent by the company to a customer would be evidence of a debit to accounts receivable and a credit to inventory. An invoice received by the company from a supplier would be evidence of a debit to inventory and a credit to accounts payable.

The journal records each transaction on one line, with the date and a name or reference to the original document. Debits and credits are posted in various accounts, with a separate column for each account. In order to avoid an unwieldy document with 24 or more columns, it is customary to divide the journal into several specialized journals with one for accounts payable, one for cash disbursements, one for cash receipts and sales.

Sales of goods to customers and payments received from customers would be recorded in journal entries like this:

CASH RECEIPTS AND SALES JOURNAL

| Date | Source | Acct. No. | Cash Received | Accounts Receivable | | Sales |
				Debit	Credit	
Feb. 15	J. Smith & Co.	AR-1		$ 60.00		$ 60.00
Feb. 20	J. Jones & Co.	AR-2		300.00		300.00
Feb. 21	Cash sale		$ 40.00			40.00
Feb. 25	J. Smith & Co.	AR-1	60.00		$ 60.00	
			$100.00	$360.00	$ 60.00	$400.00

Page CR-1

22

The first entry shows that goods were shipped to customer Smith, with a debit to accounts receivable. Then Smith paid his bill on February 25. The second entry shows goods shipped to customer Jones and the third entry shows a cash sale to a customer whose name is not recorded.

Note that this journal is in balance, since the debits in the first two columns total $460.00 and the credits in the last two columns also total $460.00.

The next step is the ledger. Here is how the above journal totals (but not the separate entries) would be entered in various ledgers, with a separate ledger for each account:

CASH

Date	Source	DR.	CR.	Balance
Feb. 25	CR-1	$ 100.00		

ACCOUNTS RECEIVABLE

Date	Source	DR.	CR.	Balance
Feb. 25	CR-1	$ 360.00	$ 60.00	$300.00 DR

All of the separate ledgers are combined into a general ledger, with each account ledger on a separate page. In a large company, the general ledger may be in several volumes.

The next step in the sequence is a trial balance, which is a listing of all of the ledger account balances to make sure that the general ledger is in balance:

TRIAL BALANCE

February 25, 1980

ACCT. NO.	ACCOUNT	DEBIT	CREDIT
A-1	Cash	$100.00	
A-2	Accounts Receivable	300.00	
A-3	Inventory	300.00	
A-4	Plant, Property & Equipment	1,000.00	
L-1	Accounts Payable		$100.00
C-1	Common Stock		500.00
I-1	Sales		1,500.00
E-1	Purchases	300.00	
E-2	Labor	100.00	
		$2,100.00	$2,100.00

The next step is adjusting entries. These appear in the general journal and are posted to the appropriate ledger accounts. They do not represent actual transactions, but are made in order to make the books more accurate, which is to say more conservative. Typical adjusting entries are transfers into the bad debt reserve, to reflect the possibility that some receivables may not be collected, and transfers into the depreciation reserve.

Another type of adjusting entry reflects expenses that have been incurred or accrued but not yet billed or paid. For example, suppose the company payday is the 1st and 15th of the month. If a balance sheet were prepared on the 10th, it would require an adjusting entry to reflect the fact that employees had worked for several days and earned wages and salaries that would be paid to them on the 15th.

The next step in the bookkeeping sequence is to prepare working papers. The working papers include the trial balance, the adjusting entries, the profit and loss statement, and the balance sheet.

To prepare working papers for a company, enter each general ledger account in the column on the left-hand side of the working papers. The account number, name, and balance are entered. Then the debit and credit columns are totaled, to confirm that they are in balance.

Next, enter the adjusting entries in their appropriate debit and credit columns. For example, adjusting entry number 1 increases the allowance for uncollectible accounts by $300, and debits bad debt expense by an equal amount. All other adjusting entries are posted in the same manner, and then totaled to make sure that they are also in balance.

At this point, we are ready to develop a profit and loss statement and a balance sheet. This is done by taking each account listed in the left-hand column, adding or subtracting any adjusting entries, and posting the result in either the profit and loss statement or balance sheet columns. All accounts that represent income and expense go into the profit and loss statement columns, while all assets, liability, or equity accounts are posted to the balance sheet columns.

The closing inventory is then entered as a credit entry in the profit and loss statement, with an equal debit entry on the balance sheet.

The profit and loss statement columns are then totaled. If the income side (credits) exceeds the expense side (debit), the difference between the two represents a profit, which is then entered in the debit column of the profit and loss statement. It is also entered in the credit column of the balance sheet as an increase to retained earnings. A loss would be a credit entry to the profit and loss statement, and a debit entry, or reduction of retained earnings, on the balance sheet.

The profit and loss columns are totaled, and should be equal. The balance sheet columns must also be equal.

ACCT. NO.	ACCOUNT	TRIAL BALANCE DEBITS		CREDITS	
A-1	Cash	4,600			
	Accounts receivable	3,000			
	Allowance for uncollectible accounts			500	
	Inventory December 1, 1979	15,000			
	Equipment	25,000			
	Allowance for depreciation			1,100	
	Accounts payable			5,000	
	Loans payable			5,000	
	Capital stock			20,000	
	Retained earnings			10,000	
	Sales			20,000	
	Purchases	8,000			
	Labor	5,000			
	Rent	1,000			
		61,600		61,600	
	Bad debt expense				
	Depreciation expense				
	Accrued salaries payable				
	Interest expense				
	Accrued interest payable				
	Inventory, December 31, 1979				
	Net income				

Chapter Four

FLOW OF FUNDS AND CASH FLOW

Every business needs an accounting system if it is to have an accurate picture of its profits--how much it is making and when. It would be nice to simply count the cash in the till at the end of the day, subtract the amount at the beginning of the day, and consider the difference to be the day's profits. But that doesn't provide an accurate measure of profits, even in the simplest of businesses, such as driving a cab or operating a shoe shine stand.

Counting cash doesn't work because of differences in timing. The business buys many goods and services on credit; they are used first and paid for later. Other goods and services are paid for in advance, which means that the cash is expended now but the benefit received later, perhaps spread over a number of years. And merchandise in inventory, whether or not it has already been paid for, may be carried over to the next year before it can be sold.

The accrual method

In order to deal with these timing differences, accounting has developed a system of accruals. The accrual method recognizes income and expenses in the period when they should properly apply, no matter when the cash was received.

We have already seen several examples of accruals. When goods are shipped to a customer, the company accrues the invoiced amount; it is recognized as an item of income and is added to accounts receivable. Later, when the customer pays the bill (which may be in the same accounting period or in a later one), the amount is added to cash, and accounts receivable are reduced accordingly.

Similarly, when the company receives a shipment of raw materials or other items on credit, it accrues an expense that will be paid later. In the meantime, until it is paid, the amount owed is recorded as an account payable, together with other accrued expenses and unpaid bills.

When an item is accrued, accountants say that there is a flow of funds, even though no cash is paid. Later, when the customer pays the bill, there is cash flow, but no flow of funds. The payment produces two offsetting changes in current assets--cash is increased and accounts receivable is reduced. But total current assets (and working capital) remain unchanged.

The balance sheet and income statement, two of the three principal accounting reports, include a number of cash items and a number of accrual items. They are combined in order to provide a meaningful and accurate presentation.

But this presentation of the income statement has the disadvantage that it obscures the company's cash position and flow of cash. The income statement shows the profits for a period but does not show whether cash on hand has been increased or reduced. And it is possible that a company may show excellent profits and yet be short of cash and unable to pay its bills as they come due. This frequently happens when business is good and management gets overoptimistic and starts running the factory at full blast. The result is big increases in inventories, accounts receivable, or both, but cash is reduced sharply. If sales don't meet expectations or if the customers are slow in paying, there may be a critical cash crunch.

The same thing can happen if the company pours large amounts into new plant and equipment and pays for it out of current resources rather than by raising new permanent capital through the sale of stock or long-term notes. In both examples the companies are asset-rich and cash-poor.

The flow of funds statement

In addition to the balance sheet and the income statement, the third of the three major accounting reports is the one that separates the cash items from accrual items in the income statement and shows how the working capital position changed during the period. It is called the flow of funds statement; alternatively, it is sometimes referred to as sources and uses of funds, or the statement of changes in financial position.

Like the income statement and unlike the balance sheet, the flow of funds statement covers a period of time, not a single instant.

The flow of funds statement is in a single column, and this is how it is

33

put together:

The top line is NET INCOME for the period	$xx,xxx
ADD: Noncash expense items--those expenses which have been deducted in arriving at net income but did not require outlays of cash--e.g., depreciation (see Chapter 7).	x,xxx
ADD: Items of cash inflow not reflected in the income statement, such as proceeds from sales of new stock or new long-term debt, or proceeds from sale of fixed assets.	xxx
This total is FUNDS AVAILABLE (that is, the total amount that has become available to the company during the period from all sources including net income).	$xx,xxx
SUBTRACT: Cash outlays not shown as expenses on the income statement. For example, purchase of fixed assets that will be depreciated in future years, payment of dividends to stockholders, repurchase of stock, and repayment of long-term debt.	xxx
The total is the NET INCREASE IN WORKING CAPITAL during the period.	$xx,xxx

Normally if the company is growing and making a profit, the last figure will be an actual increase. But not always. If the company is spending heavily for plant and equipment, current assets and working capital may decrease. A decrease could also result if the company pays out more in dividends than it earned during the period.

The rest of the flow of funds statement consists of a breakdown of the working capital change; that is, it shows the changes in the various components of current assets and current liabilities. If the company is not growing, the increase in working capital will probably show up in cash on hand. But in a rapidly growing company cash might actually decrease because funds have been used to build up inventories and receivables. By the same token, if the company has dragged its feet about paying its bills, thus

34

in effect borrowing from suppliers and creditors, the accounts payable will show an increase.

A sample flow of funds statement is shown in Appendix C.

The cash flow statement

Many managers like to have the last part of the flow of funds statement, the section showing the changes in the various components of net working capital, prepared in a different format to further highlight the changes in the cash position. This is the cash flow statement, which is not one of the basic accounting reports but is a valuable guide for management, and perhaps also for the company's bankers and other creditors. A sample cash flow statement appears in Appendix D.

The cash flow statement is often prepared on a monthly basis or perhaps even more frequently. It shows the cash balance at the end of last month, the balance at the end of this month, and exactly what acccounts for the difference; that is, which current assets and liabilities increased and which ones decreased.*

Interrelationships of the three basic reports

The three principal accounting reports--the balance sheet, income statement, and flow of funds statement--provide all of the essential information about a company's operations during a year and its financial position at the end of the year. The figures are in summary form, of course,

*The term "cash flow" is often used with a different meaning by security analysts and financial writers. They use it to mean the total of net income, depreciation, and other noncash expense items. In other words, gross cash flow. This figure does not take into account the use of the funds.

and in some instances it may be necessary to ask for more detail or a breakdown of the totals. But all the essentials are there.

These three reports form an integrated and interconnected system
that fits precisely together. Whenever a change is made in any figure in any
one of the three reports, the other two must also be changed. Otherwise the
system will be out of balance.

Management control of profits and cash flow

The outsider who analyzes the financial statements of a company
should be aware that management has some ability to adjust the figures to
make the profits look better. And occasionally a management wants to make
the picture look less favorable than it really is. (For example, a new chief
executive taking over a troubled company may want to exaggerate the problems so that the turnaround he hopes to bring about will seem a greater
achievement.)

Accounting is a fairly exact discipline, but management has some latitude in determining how it presents the figures. Here are some of the discretionary adjustments that can be made:

• Timing of expenditures. If an expense can be postponed until the
next accounting period, the profit picture for the current period will
look better at the expense of the next period. Sometimes management will do
the opposite and accelerate an expense from next year into this year. (For
example, when this year's earnings are very high and it is known that next
year won't be as good, the company may wish to reduce this year's profits
and increase next year's to moderate the year-to-year change.)

• Deferred maintenance is a particularly dangerous form of postponed expenses. Management may delay making needed repairs to plant and equipment in order to make current profits look better. The result may be that the repairs cost more when they are ultimately made, and equipment may suffer permanent damage. Excessive deferral of maintenance may be a sign that a company's owners are milking it.

• Capitalizing repairs. Routine maintenance and repairs are charged off as a current expense. But if a machine or building is extensively overhauled or rebuilt, it may be appropriate to treat the cost in the same way as if new equipment had been bought. In accounting terms, that means "capitalizing" it, carrying it on the balance sheet as a fixed asset and depreciating it over many years. In borderline cases management has some latitude in deciding whether repairs will be expensed or capitalized. If this discretion is abused it can distort the profit picture by spreading an expense over many years instead of taking it in a single year.

• Excess asset lives. Management may choose excessively long estimated useful lives (Chapter 7) for fixed assets, which results in lower depreciation charges--and thus higher profits. Later, the equipment may become obsolete and have to be written off and sold for scrap before it is fully depreciated, producing lower profits in the year it is done.

• Bad debt reserves. The amount deducted from earnings and placed in the bad debt reserve may be increased or decreased, within the limits of reason, at the discretion of management. The effect can be to generate artificial increases or decreases in profits and stated asset values.

Reputable business managers often consider that it is appropriate to use these discretionary adjustments to even out year-to-year fluctuations in profits, since wide profit swings are disturbing to stockholders, lenders, and others who rely on the financial statements. Some managements are less scrupulous and deliberately use these discretionary adjustments to manipulate earnings.

An investor or financial analyst who is not a member of the management group will generally not be able to find out what adjustments have been made. Occasionally there will be a clue in the notes to the financial statements or in the text of a report to stockholders, but this is rare. Usually the adjustments can be uncovered only by extensive questioning of the financial officers and the outside auditors, or by retaining an independent CPA firm to make a complete audit of the books.

Chapter Five

ANALYZING THE FINANCIAL STATEMENTS

The three basic financial statements present all of the essential financial information about the company and its operations for the most recent year or other accounting period. They constitute an essential tool for management. In addition, they are indispensable for those outside the company who want to understand its financial situation.

But this kind of understanding requires analysis; in order to draw conclusions about a company's financial soundness and profitability, and to compare it with other companies, it is necessary to compare certain figures in the various statements with others and to compute certain ratios and relationships. Some useful ratios can be calculated from a single statement, but many of the important ones involve parts of two or more statements--for example, comparing certain balance sheet figures with income statement figures, or examining income or flow of funds statements covering five years.

Creditors vs. investors

What is the analyst looking for? That depends on his point of view, and there are two basic approaches to financial analysis. One is the creditor's viewpoint; the other approach is that of the equity investor, or owner. These two approaches are very different and in some respects they are opposed to each other. That is, some figures and ratios which would give great comfort to a creditor would be viewed as unfavorable by an equity investor, and vice versa.

The creditor's analysis

The use of financial statements as a basis for extending credit is second in importance only to their use as a management tool. The creditor may be:

- A supplier who ships goods to the company on credit.

- A bank officer considering extending a line of credit or a loan to the company.

- A property owner who may rent office, warehouse, or factory space to the company, or who may sell property to the company and take back a mortgage.

- A bond investor who may make a loan to the company, either directly or by buying its publicly traded bonds in the market. (Note that this investor has a very different point of view from that of the equity investor or stockholder.)

The creditor's concern is very simple. He wants the company to pay

what is due, including interest, and pay it all on time without any problems. He doesn't want payments to be late, he doesn't want to hear excuses,
and above all he does not want the company to default on what it owes him or
go bankrupt and default on what it owes to everybody.

Of course, the creditor understands that there is always some risk
that a borrowing business may run into difficulties. And he is willing to
take some risk. But he wants to measure the risk as accurately as possible,
and to ask the "what if" questions. Will the company still be able to pay its
bills if there is a recession? A strike? If its just introduced new product
bombs out? If its autocratic, hard-driving president suddenly becomes
disabled or dies?

Among the figures that the creditor considers most important and
informative are:

- The current ratio.
- The quick ratio, or acid test.
- The debt-to-equity ratio.

The current ratio

The ratio of current assets (cash and assets that will be turned into
cash within 12 months) to current liabilities (obligations that will be
paid within 12 months) is called the current ratio. It is considered one of
the key indicators of the company's ability to pay its bills on time.

Creditors generally consider a current ratio of two to one or higher
to be desirable. (The common usage is to state only the higher number. It
would be said that the current ratio is 2.34 if current assets equalled 234
percent of current liabilities.)

The quick ratio or acid test

Creditors consider the current ratio to be important, but it leaves something to be desired, since current assets include inventory. If the company's sales suddenly slowed it might be unable to liquidate inventory and raise cash. Thus, creditors also like to look at what they call the quick assets ratio, which is the ratio of current assets excluding inventory to current liabilities. Or, to put it another way, the ratio of the total of cash, marketable securities, and receivables to current liabilities. In common parlance the quick assets ratio is usually referred to as the quick ratio. It is also called the acid test. A quick ratio of 1.0 or higher is considered very satisfactory.

Capitalization ratio or ratio of debt to equity

Financial analysts make a distinction between short-term or current liabilities and long-term liabilities such as mortgages, bonds, or other obligations repayable over more than one year. The longer-term liabilities represent money available to the company for an extended period; long-term liabilities plus equity funds are considered the capitalization or capital structure of the company. The new balance sheet format (page 16) highlights this figure, calling it funds employed in the business.

In examining the capitalization, the creditor is vitally concerned about the balance between the debt and equity components. If the company suffers reverses, the equity provides a cushion for the creditors. If it loses money, the losses will reduce the equity. If it loses a lot of money, so much that the equity is wiped out, the creditors will worry about whether long-term debt can be repaid.

But it isn't only the holders of long-term debt who worry. The short-term creditors get nervous, too. If the company should go bankrupt, with assets (when liquidated) insufficient to pay all liabilities, it is likely that most or all of the creditors will be treated equally, with each receiving only a fraction, perhaps a small fraction, of what is owed. And, if the long-term debt is secured, the short-term creditors may end up with less than the long-term ones, even though their claims were prior in time.

In practice, the degree of concern differs according to the kind of business: in manufacturing companies, creditors usually like to see long-term debt at no more than 33 1/3 percent of capitalization. To put it another way, they like to see equity equal to 200 percent of long-term debt. And there is likely to be serious concern if debt exceeds 50 percent of capitalization. Different standards apply in other industries; much higher debt ratios are acceptable for a finance company or a utility.

The equity investor's analysis

If the creditor likes the idea of lending to a rich company, a fat company with lots of cash and assets to provide a cushion or a margin for error or adversity, the equity investor by contrast prefers a lean company, one that works its assets harder and produces the maximum return on them. If the company has a high current ratio and a high quick ratio, the creditor is pleased, but the equity investor may not like it at all. His attitude may be, "Management, why are you sitting on all that cash instead of investing it to produce more earnings? Do you think you're running a bank?"

Among the figures that are most important to the equity investor are:

• Return on investment.

- Leverage.

- Return on sales.

- Capital intensivity.

Return on investment (ROI)

The equity investor wants the company to use his money to make more money, and as much more as possible. He is more interested in profits than in sales. A company that achieves a billion dollars or ten billion in sales is not necessarily a good investment just because of those mammoth numbers, since it may be sacrificing profits to build sales. But even the size of profits is not the basic criterion. The really important figure is profits in relation to invested capital--or return on investment.

We have seen that the capitalization, also called the funds employed in the business, is in two parts: long-term debt and equity. The financial analyst considers a key measure of management strength to be its ability to earn as much profit as possible every year on the money invested.

Suppose a company had equity capital (common stock, capital surplus, and retained earnings) at the end of 1979 of $1,000,000. If during 1980 the company earns $200,000 of net income after taxes, that is a 20 percent return on investment.

Not bad, but investors would say the rate of return should be measured against other investments with a similar amount of risk. If a company has an ROI of 10 percent, and government bonds yield 12 percent, the company is not using its assets efficiently.

The following chart, one of the "Executive Committee Control Charts" of the du Pont Company, shows all of the factors which affect ROI:

44

FORMULA CHART
Relationship of Factors Affecting Return on Investment

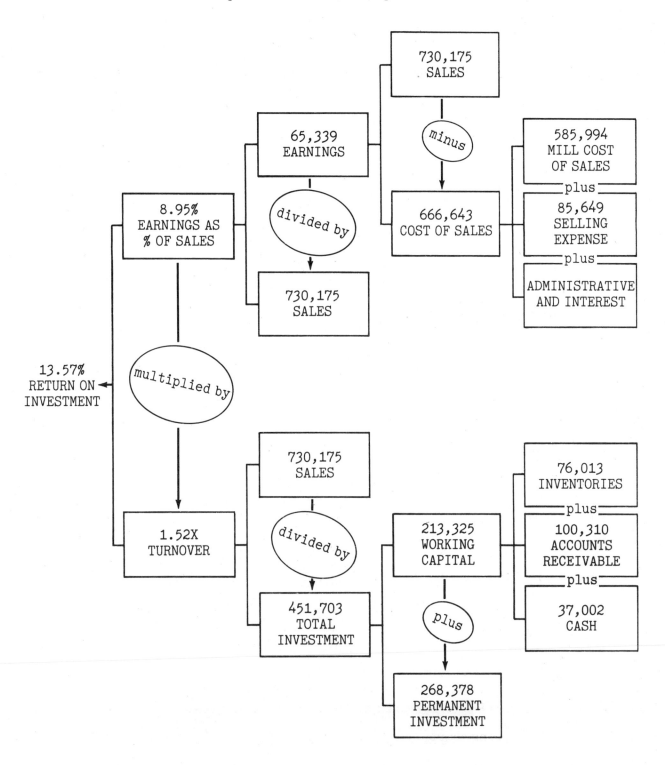

The ROI analysis is extremely valuable when applied to the company's total results, but it is also useful--indeed, critical--in appraising an individual product line or capital expenditure project. When managment examines a proposed new product or new venture, the key question is: what ROI can we expect? How much do we have to invest in this venture, and what return will it bring if we meet our projections?

Similarly, in reviewing an existing product or project that is doing poorly and may be dropped, management asks how much capital would be released for other uses if the project were scrapped and whether a better return could be earned elsewhere.

Leverage: The key to investors' profits

The company that earned $200,000 on $1,000,000 of all-equity capitalization might be criticized by its stockholders for being too conservative. They might feel that management should negotiate long-term borrowings and increase the company's capital base so as to produce additional earnings, and do it without requiring additional investment of equity funds.

For example, suppose that this same company had, over the years, paid more in dividends and retained less earnings, so that its equity investment was only $650,000 rather than $1,000,000. But it had negotiated long-term borrowings of $350,000. Thus its debt would be 35 percent of capitalization.

If the money were borrowed at 10 percent, the annual interest cost would be $35,000 before taxes and about $20,000 after taxes. Thus profits after taxes would be reduced from $200,000 to about $180,000. But the return on equity would be improved; $180,000 of net after taxes is a 27.7 percent return on the $650,000 of equity, compared to 20 percent in the no-debt situation.

This is leverage. It is the use of borrowings to increase the return on equity. Investors are more concerned with profits than with safety, and thus they like to see their company use leverage (that is, borrow) as much as possible--within reason. If the company has debt, increases in profits produce greater percentage increases in the return on equity.

With leverage, the investor's pulse quickens when he contemplates a possible big periodic increase in income.

If he looks at two companies--one with a high debt/equity ratio and one with a low debt/equity ratio--a dollar change in preinterest income will result in a greater percentage change in net income for the company with the high debt/equity ratio. Suppose the two companies each have $1 million in capital, but one is much more highly leveraged than the other:

	Low Debt/ Equity-10/90	High Debt/ Equity-60/40
BASE PERIOD		
Preinterest Income	$100,000	$100,000
Interest @ 10%	10,000	60,000
Pretax Income	$ 90,000	$ 40,000
HIGH INCOME PERIOD		
Preinterest Income	$300,000	$300,000
Interest @ 10%	10,000	60,000
Pretax Income	$290,000	$240,000
% Change in Pretax Income from a 300% increase in Pre- interest Income	322%	600%

Of course, leverage works both ways. When profits drop, the return on equity drops much faster in a leveraged company (one that has sizable debt). Indeed, it is possible that a leveraged company could show a small operating profit that turns into a loss after interest is deducted.

Return on sales

Although the return on investment is the most important figure to the equity investor, he also looks at return on sales. He is more impressed with the profitability of sales than with the volume. A company that slashes prices to the bone to build volume may grow enormously and make a big splash, but it is merely "trading dollars" without making much profit.

A well-managed manufacturing company can usually bring ten cents of every sales dollar down to pretax profit; that is, its return on sales would be about ten percent before income taxes and just over five percent after taxes. Retailers generally show a lower return on sales--perhaps only three to four percent before income taxes. And major grocery chains earn only one percent or so, some even less.

Another important aspect of return on sales is the gross margin. As discussed on page 29, gross profit is the profit after deducting cost of goods sold but before deducting selling, administrative, and other expenses. The gross margin is the relationship between gross profit and total sales. For manufacturing companies, gross margins usually range between 20 and 35 percent. Again, they are lower for retailers.

Capital intensiveness

Some industries are referred to as capital intensive, which means that they have large investments in plant facilities. Examples are steel, oil refining, cement, and copper mining. Usually such companies have a high proportion of their total assets invested in fixed assets--probably 50 percent or more.

And they usually have annual sales equal to only 20 percent to 40 percent of their fixed assets. To put it another way, it takes several dollars' worth of fixed assets to produce a dollar of sales--about ten cents in pretax profits.

Capital intensive industries have the advantage that new competitors are discouraged from entering the business because the required initial investment is large. But the return on investment is likely to be relatively low, even if the company is highly leveraged. Thus, many investors prefer to avoid capital intensive companies.

Control and other ratios

Certain other accounting ratios, affecting a range of matters from depreciation to accounts receivable, are important to management in keeping control of operations and monitoring the company's financial efficiency. They are also of interest to both creditors and equity investors, although they are perhaps less crucial the ratios that were discussed earlier.

Depreciation/total plant

If the depreciation reserve represents a high percentage of total gross fixed assets, it tends to indicate that the company's plant and equipment are old and may need modernizing. (Analysts must use caution in comparing this ratio for different companies, because they may be using different rates and methods of depreciation.)

Working capital per dollar of sales

A well-managed company tries to work its investment dollars as hard as possible and to get as many sales dollars as possible out of each dollar of working capital. If sales are $1,000,000 and net working capital is $170,000, then the company has 17 cents of working capital for every dollar of sales. And if it plans to increase sales by, say 20 percent, it will need another $34,000 of working capital (20 percent of $170,000) to support the the higher sales.

Inventory turnover

The ratio between annual sales and inventory on hand shows how fast the company turns over its inventory. Some manufacturing companies have inventories equaling as high as 20 percent or 25 percent of sales, which means that their inventory turns over only four or five times a year. Retailers, especially food chains and high-volume discounters, may turn their inventory over 20 times or more, so that their inventory is only five percent or less of annual sales. Obviously a high turnover is preferable; if the company can increase its turnover it can use its invested dollars more efficiently and increase its return on investment.

Receivable collection period

In order to determine how long it takes to collect from the average customer, this formula is used:

$$\frac{\text{Accounts Receivable}}{\text{Net Sales}} \quad \text{x} \quad 365$$

For example: $\frac{\$140,000}{\$1,000,000} = \frac{14}{100} \text{ x } 365 = 51.1 \text{ days}$

Some customers pay faster than this and others more slowly, but the average receivable is collected in 51.1 days. Comparison with other companies in the same industry may show that one company has a higher figure than others, which would indicate that its collection efforts need attention.

Days payable outstanding

This formula shows how long the company takes to pay its bills:

$$\frac{\text{Accounts payable}}{\text{Costs of goods sold}} \quad \text{x} \quad 365 \quad = \quad \text{Days payable outstanding}$$

$$\frac{\$100,000}{\$1,000,000} = \frac{1}{10} \text{ x } 36.5 \text{ days}$$

Management will try to keep its receivable collection period as short as possible, without antagonizing customers by undue collection pressure. By contrast, it would like its outstanding payable period to be as long as possible without endangering the company's credit rating by slow payment.

Tax rate

The tax rate is calculated by taking income taxes as a percentage of pretax income. For very large companies, the rate will usually be 46 percent (the federal maximum) or perhaps around 50 percent for companies located in states with high corporate income tax rates.

If a large company's income tax rate is significantly below 46 per cent, there are several possible explanations:

- It may be taking faster depreciation on its tax returns than on its financial statements as reported to stockholders.

- It may have operations in Puerto Rico or some other tax-favored location.

- It may have depletion or other tax advantages. For example, sale of timber by a lumber company produces capital gains rather than ordinary income.

- Losses in past years may have been used to offset the current year's profits and thus reduce taxes.

In all of these situations, especially the last one, the analyst must inquire whether the unusual tax situation is about to come to an end. If so, the tax rate can be expected to increase and net income will be reduced accordingly.

Trend analysis

Much meaningful information about the company's progress (or lack of it) can be gleaned from a comparison of financial ratios over a period of time. For example:

- If the return on investment is dropping, it may be a cause for alarm, possibly indicating a need for major changes in management personnel or policies, unless it is known to be caused by a temporary difficulty.

- If inventory turnover drops, it may indicate that management has failed to adjust production to declining sales in some product lines.

- An increase in the receivable collection period, especially if it is combined with increases in the charge-off of bad debts, may be a sign

52

that management is trying to build (or maintain) sales by loosening credit standards and by selling to customers whose credit is shaky.

A very important factor to be remembered in the analysis of financial statement ratios is that only like items should be compared. In examining the statements of two companies, comparisons will not be valid unless they both have the same items in each account and use the same accounting methods. And, in comparing results for different years for the same company, adjustments must be made for any changes in accounting policies or procedures during the period.

Chapter Six

INVENTORIES

Inventory is one of the most important items on the typical balance sheet. And cost of goods sold is often the largest single expense item on the income statement. For a manufacturing company, cost of goods sold includes amounts paid for raw materials and component parts as well as the cost of processing and manufacturing, including labor, supplies, power, and depreciation of machinery. For a wholesaler or retailer, on the other hand, cost of goods sold consists almost entirely of the purchase cost of the finished goods.

Inventory and cost of goods sold are major factors in determining a company's profitability. The accounting treatment of these items is extremely complicated and offers management a good deal of flexibility. It can make a number of choices that can have important effects upon both profits and balance sheet values.

Inventory includes:

• Finished goods--items that are held for sale in the ordinary course of business. They may have been produced by a manufacturing company or acquired for resale by a retailer.

• Work in process--items that are in the process of production for such sale.

• Raw materials and supplies--expected to be consumed in the production of goods and services for sale.

Various methods of inventory accounting can produce different levels of profits, even though the physical volume of inventory does not change. For example:

	Low Inventory Level	High Inventory Level
Net sales	$100,000	$100,000
Cost of goods sold:		
Purchases	30,000	30,000
Manufacturing expense	20,000	20,000
Goods available for sale	$ 50,000	$ 50,000
Less: closing inventory	10,000	15,000
Cost of goods sold	40,000	35,000
Gross profit	$ 60,000	$ 65,000
Other expenses	40,000	40,000
Profit before taxes	$ 20,000	$ 25,000

(Note that manufacturing expenses such as supervision, maintenance, and depreciation are included in cost of goods sold.)

An inventory valuation method that produces high values also maximizes profits. If the method produces low values, it minimizes taxable profits and, accordingly, income taxes.

Lower of cost or market

Assets are generally carried on the balance sheet at cost. But sometimes it is necessary to reduce the stated value to reflect the conservative philosophy that is essential in accounting. For example, suppose a manufacturer or retailer guesses wrong about consumer preferences and ends up with sizable inventories of goods like gas-guzzling cars, pet rocks, or Nehru jackets, items that cannot be sold except at distress prices. If the market value of the inventory falls, not only below the previously anticipated selling price but also below cost, then the company should mark down the inventory to its actual market value, rather than carrying it at cost.

Thus, inventory is carried at original cost or market value, whichever is lower. In common usage this principle is expressed as "lower of cost or market." If market values rise as a result of inflation or for other reasons, the stated value of the inventory remains the same. (While it's not marked up then, of course, the higher value will be recognized at the time the inventory is sold.)

Methods of inventory valuation

In general, accounting practice requires that items in inventory be valued individually rather than as a single total. However, it is permissible in inventory valuation to group together all identical or closely similar items--for example, all men's winter suits of various sizes, or

56

all pieces of sheet steel.

First-in, first-out--FIFO

One inventory valuation method assumes that the items purchased or produced first are the first items to be used or sold. That is, first units in are first out. The commonly used abbreviation for this method of valuation is FIFO.

To visualize FIFO, imagine a factory with an assembly line running from the front of the building to the back. Raw materials and components are unloaded at the front door, placed on the assembly line, and processed as they move along it toward the back of the building. There, the finished goods are shipped out to customers. Those materials that arrive first at the front will be the first to be shipped out the back in the form of manufactured products.

Last-in, first-out--LIFO

In contrast to FIFO is the last-in, first-out method which assumes that the last items acquired or produced are the first to be used or sold. The common abbreviation for this method is LIFO. An easy way to visualize LIFO is to imagine a coal pile, with new deliveries dumped on top and coal shoveled off the top of the pile as it is used. The coal that was delivered most recently is used first, then the previous delivery is used, and so on. The first coal that was received stays at the bottom of the pile and may never be used, as long as some coal remains on top of the pile.

The following table shows the different results of using FIFO and LIFO on the same sequence of purchases and production:

	Units received			Units used in production FIFO			LIFO		
	Units	Price	Total Cost	Units	Price	Total Cost	Units	Price	Total Cost
1/2	1,000	$.20	$ 200						
1/9	2,000	.22	440						
1/10				2,500 units used, consisting of:					
				1,000	$.20	$ 200	2,000	$.22	$ 440
				1,500	.22	330	500	.20	100
1/16	2,000	.24	480						
1/17				2,000 units used, consisting of:					
				500	.22	110	2,000	.24	480
				1,600	.24	384	100	.20	20
1/23	2,000	.24	480						
1/24	1,000	.24	480	1,000	.24	480			
1/30	1,000	.26	260						
1/31				1,300 units used, consisting of:					
				1,300	.24	312	1,000	.26	260
							300	.24	72
Total purchases			$1,860	Cost of goods		$1,576			$1,612
Opening inventory				0		0	0		0
Closing inventory				100	.24	24	400	.20	80
				1,000	.26	260	700	.24	168
				1,100		284	1,100		248

	FIFO	LIFO
Opening inventory	$ 0	$ 0
Plus: Purchases	1,860	1,860
Goods available for use	$1,860	$1,860
Less: Closing inventory	284	148
Cost of goods sold	$1,576	$1,612

During the period shown, which was a period of rising prices, LIFO produced a higher cost of goods sold and hence lower profits (and lower income taxes) than FIFO. The reverse would be true in a period of falling prices.

Note that the closing inventory under LIFO was valued at a lower figure, since it consisted of the units purchased first. (Those purchased later had all been used.) If prices rise continuously for a long period,

LIFO produces a drastic understatement of inventory values. If a strike or some other unusual event caused all of the old and low-valued inventory to be used, the company would generate very large profits--and very large income taxes.

Many companies have switched to LIFO in recent years as a response to continuing inflation. This has produced a significant saving in income taxes. However, if prices should drop for an extended period, taxes would be considerably higher under LIFO.

An inventory method that is perhaps more logical than either FIFO or LIFO is the weighted average method. That is, the inventory of identical units is valued at the average cost of all units on hand. If the weighted average had been used in the table, the closing inventory would have been $272.64 and the cost of goods sold $1,587.36. However, the weighted average method, logical though it may be, is rarely the one employed by larger companies.

The retail method

In a retail store, goods are marked with price tags showing selling price rather than cost. For this reason, taking inventory would be extremely burdensome if it were necessary to check original invoices to determine the cost of each item. As a result, accounting practice and the Internal Revenue Service approve the use of the retail method, which takes the store's normal markup and applies it to all merchandise that is held for sale.

For example, suppose a store marks its average item up by $66\frac{2}{3}$ percent for retail sale. An item costing 60 cents would be priced at $1.00, and one costing $3.00 would be priced at $5.00.

If the percentage is calculated based on the selling price rather than the cost, it is said that the store has a 40 percent margin. Its gross profit is 40 cents, or 40 percent, on the $1.00 item and $2.00 on the $5.00 item.

The retail inventory valuation method would apply this 40 percent margin to the total value of all the price tags in the store. If the inventory was worth $50,000, based on the price tags, that figure would be reduced by 40 percent to produce an inventory value of $30,000.

Other inventory valuation methods

Certain other inventory methods, though not acceptable for financial statements or tax returns, are valuable to management for control and planning purposes. For example, replacement cost of inventory is an extremely important figure in a time of steadily rising prices, when goods may sometimes be sold at a profit but at a lower price than it would cost the merchant to replace them. (For a brief period in late 1979 and early 1980, Tiffany was selling sterling silver below replacement cost. The items had been manufactured and purchased by the store when silver was selling at $6 to $8 per ounce, and retail prices had not been adjusted to reflect the silver price of $35 to $45 per ounce that was reached late in 1979.)

Occasionally, management will use HIFO (highest-in, first-out) or NIFO (next-in, first-out). NIFO is essentially the same as valuing inventory on a replacement cost basis. Both these methods assume that all cost increases are permanent and that prices will not go down.

A company bidding on a contract to supply goods at a future date is well advised to calculate its bid based on estimated future cost of acquiring inventory, rather than on historical costs which may not recur.

Supplies: Expense vs. inventory

A slightly different inventory treatment may be used for consumable supplies--those items that are used up in the production process or otherwise to maintain the physical plant and operate the business. For example: grease, welding rods, light bulbs, adding machine paper, detergent compound for cleaning the floor. It is not practical to count sheets of paper or measure half-used drums of cleaning compound every time inventory is taken. Therefore, it is customary to charge off the full cost of consumable supplies that will be used in a short period of time.

We have seen that management has considerable flexibility in determining the valuation of inventory. Management decisions which increase the cost of inventory used (such as adopting LIFO) have the effect of reducing profits and income taxes. And they also reduce the value of inventory on hand. Such a company may have balance sheet values that are significantly understated; accordingly, it may have the potential for large future profits when those undervalued inventories are sold. That might occur in the ordinary course of business over a period of time, or it might happen all at once if the entire company is sold or liquidated.

The choice of inventory valuation method is an important one that involves many considerations. Expert tax and accounting practitioners should be consulted in the original choice and also when it may appear appropriate to change methods. Once a particular method has been used in tax returns, it generally may not be changed without prior IRS approval.

61

Chapter Seven

FIXED ASSETS
AND DEPRECIATION

We have seen that one of the most important techniques used to present

an accurate and realistic picture of the financial results is the capital-

ization of fixed assets. When a building or machine is purchased, it would

be misleading to charge all of the cost against operations in that year

since the asset will be used for many years. And so the cost is capitalized

--it is put on the balance sheet to be recovered over a number of years

through depreciation charges to income every year.

Depreciation deserves a detailed analysis because it can be both a

major expense item and an important determinant of profits. And it can pro-

duce substantial tax savings. But it can also give rise to a great deal of

confusion and misunderstanding because of the variety of depreciation

rates and methods that may be used. Management has a good deal of freedom

and flexibility to choose among these methods; the choices made can have significant effects upon profits.

When comparing the financial statements of two companies, it is possible to draw inaccurate conclusions if one does not know that they use different depreciation rates and methods. And a single company can drastically adjust its reported income--either up or down--by certain changes in depreciation rates and methods. If the analyst does not know what changes have been made, he may be seriously misled about the level and trend of the company's profits.

Depreciation is a noncash expense, a bookkeeping entry that appears as an expense on the income statement but does not require any cash outlay. (The cash was expended earlier, when the item was purchased.) Even so, depreciation and the choice of depreciation methods and rates can importantly affect the company's cash position because of its effect upon taxes.

For example:

	High Depreciation	Low Depreciation
Income before depreciation	$100,000	$100,000
Less: Depreciation	10,000	5,000
Net taxable income	$ 90,000	$ 95,000
Income taxes @ 50%	45,000	47,500
Net income after taxes	$ 45,000	$ 47,500
Plus: Depreciation	10,000	5,000
Funds from operations	$ 55,000	$ 52,500

By taking $5,000 more in depreciation, which does not require spending a single dollar in real cash, the company can increase its flow of funds by $2,500 (the amount of the increase times the income tax rate of 50 percent). For this reason, most companies try to charge as much depreciation as they can on their income statements as reported to the Internal Revenue Service.

The amount of depreciation that will be charged each year on a particular fixed asset is a function of:

- The cost base of the asset.

- The estimated salvage value when it is scrapped or retired.

- The estimated useful life.

Cost base and salvage value

When a fixed asset is acquired, its cost is capitalized and carried on
the balance sheet. The stated balance sheet figure includes:

- Actual construction cost, if it is a building.

- Actual cost of any machinery and equipment, less any discounts or
rebates.

- Freight and delivery charges.

- Installation costs, if any, including labor.

- Interest paid during the construction period on money borrowed to
finance construction. Also interest paid, while awaiting delivery, on any
money borrowed to make down payments or progress payments.

- Insurance on the asset during construction and installation.

If the asset is a building, the cost base will include the cost of the
land. Obviously, land doesn't wear out and therefore it is not depreciated. It is carried at cost on the balance sheet indefinitely, or until it
is sold or abandoned.

Accounting practice generally requires that salvage value be taken
into account in determining depreciation. That is, it is assumed that even
when the item is worn out it will not be totally worthless. It can probably
be sold to a junk dealer or broken up for scrap. The financial officer must

make a good faith estimate--which really isn't much more than a guess in some cases--as to what the scrap or salvage value will be. Salvage value is the estimated proceeds of selling the worn-out asset after deducting any costs of dismantling and removing it.

The salvage value is subtracted from the cost base to give the net depreciable value that will be written off over the estimated useful life of the item.

Useful life

In order to determine how much of the depreciable value will be charged off each year, the company estimates how long the asset can be expected to be used for the purpose for which it was acquired. The useful life may be as short as two or three years for a pickup truck or as long as 30 or 40 years for a building.

The estimated useful life may take into account obsolescence as well as physical wear and tear--that is, some items may become obsolete and hence unusable before they are physically worn out.

The estimated useful life is determined by the company, perhaps with the assistance of engineers or accountants, based on past experience with similar assets. And the Internal Revenue Service prescribes useful lives for individual assets and also for classes of assets. Companies may take separate depreciation for each piece of equipment or they may reduce the bookkeeping by grouping assets into a class. For example, all machinery and equipment used in manufacturing pulp and paper can be treated as a class and charged off over a period as long as 15½ years, as short as 10½ years, or anything in between.

Usually, but not always, the IRS will accept the estimated useful life chosen by the company. Most companies prefer to elect a useful life as short as possible in order to maximize depreciation in the early years and thus minimize taxable income and taxes. The IRS will sometimes challenge the life as being too short and require that a longer estimated useful life be selected.

After determining the net depreciable value of the asset (that is, the cost base minus the salvage value) and the estimated useful life, the amount of depreciation that is to be charged off each year will depend on which depreciation method is being used. The three most commonly used methods are:

- Straight line.
- Declining balance.
- Sum of the years' digits.

Straight line depreciation

Straight line depreciation is the easiest to understand and to calculate. It simply spreads the depreciation uniformly over the useful life. Thus, if a machine cost $11,000 and has an estimated salvage value of $1,000, with an estimated useful life of ten years, the annual depreciation charge would be:

$$\frac{\$11,000 - \$1,000}{10 \text{ years}} = \$1,000 \text{ per year}$$

Each year $1,000 is charged to cost of goods sold for depreciation of this machine. And the value of the machine on the balance sheet is reduced by $1,000 each year:

| | | Opening | | Closing | |
Year	Book value	Depreciation reserve	Depreciation charge	Depreciation reserve	Book value
1	$11,000	$ 0	$1,000	$ 1,000	$10,000
2	10,000	1,000	1,000	2,000	9,000
3	9,000	2,000	1,000	3,000	8,000
4	8,000	3,000	1,000	4,000	7,000
5	7,000	4,000	1,000	5,000	6,000
6	6,000	5,000	1,000	6,000	5,000
7	5,000	6,000	1,000	7,000	4,000
8	4,000	7,000	1,000	8,000	3,000
9	3,000	8,000	1,000	9,000	2,000
10	2,000	9,000	1,000	10,000	1,000

At the end of the tenth year, the value of the machine on the balance sheet is the estimated salvage value, or $1,000.

While the straight line method is easy to calculate, it has certain disadvantages. It is not entirely realistic, since the actual decline in value probably does not proceed on a uniform straight line basis. Rather, most assets decline more rapidly in value in the first few years and more slowly after that. However, in later years the cost of maintenance and repairs is likely to be higher. Thus, straight line depreciation probably understates the decline in value in the earlier years and overstates it in later years.

Another problem is that straight line depreciation may not reflect the actual rate of wear and tear. For example, business may be slow in one year and the machine may stand idle much of the time. The next year, if sales and hence production pick up, it may be operating almost continuously and will suffer substantially more real depreciation. Yet the straight line method would produce exactly the same depreciation charge for both years.

A depreciation method that takes this problem into account is the unit-of-production method. It can be used, however, only if the operation of the equipment can be closely correlated with production, so that the depreciation allowance can vary according to the number of units actually produced:

$$\text{Depreciation expense} = \frac{\text{Cost} - \text{Salvage value}}{\text{Total production units}}$$

For example, if a mold is purchased for $10,000, has no salvage value, and can produce 100,000 units before having to be replaced, the depreciation expense for each unit would be:

$$\frac{10,000 - 0}{100,000} = \$.10/\text{unit}$$

The annual depreciation expense and book value of the mold would be:

Year	Production units	Depreciation expense	End of year Depreciation reserve	Book value
1	25,000	$2,500	$ 2,500	$7,500
2	30,000	3,000	5,500	4,500
3	25,000	2,500	8,000	2,000
4	10,000	1,000	9,000	1,000
5	10,000	1,000	10,000	0

When 100,000 units have been produced, the entire cost of the mold will have been expensed, and if the estimate of its useful life was correct, it will then have no value and will have to be replaced.

Declining balance

Many companies prefer to use accelerated depreciation methods which permit depreciation deductions larger than straight line in the early years and smaller than straight line in later years. Declining balance is one accelerated depreciation method. It simply increases the percentage written off each year and then applies that percentage to the declining balance that remains in future years. The result is a depreciation schedule that starts higher and then declines steadily.

Because the IRS permits taking as much as 200 percent, or double the straight line percentage, a popular depreciation method is double declining balance. (Salvage value is not taken into account in the declining balance method.)

Here is a comparison of straight line and double declining balance depreciation on the same $11,000 machine:

Year	Opening Book Value	Straight Line Depreci- ation	Rate	X	Multiple	=	Declining Balance Rate	Depreciation	Closing Book Value
1	$11,000	$1,000	10%	X	200%	=	20%	$ 2,200	$9,800
2	9,800	$1,000	10%	X	200%	=	20%	1,960	7,840
3	7,840	$1,000	10%	X	200%	=	20%	1,568	6,272
4	6,272	$1,000	10%	X	200%	=	20%	1,254	5,018
5	5,018	$1,000	10%	X	200%	=	20%	1,004	4,014
6	4,014	$1,000	10%	X	200%	=	20%	803	3,211
7	3,211	$1,000	10%	X	200%	=	20%	642	2,569
8	2,569	$1,000	10%	X	200%	=	20%	514	2,055
9	2,055	$1,000	10%	X	200%	=	20%	411	1,644
10	1,644	$1,000	10%	X	200%	=	20%	328	1,315

(Note that the straight line calculation uses a depreciable value of $10,000, because salvage value is deducted, but the double declining balance method does not take salvage value into account; thus it applies the percentage to the full $11,000 cost in the first year.)

With the declining balance method, it is usually not possible to end up with a net book value equaling the salvage value. In order to accomplish this, a company may change from the declining balance method to the straight line method at any time.

If, at the end of Year 6, the company changed to the straight line method, it would have then calculated the remaining depreciation as:

$$\text{Annual Depreciation} = \frac{\text{Net Book Value-Salvage Value}}{\text{Remaining Life}}$$

$$= \frac{3,211 - 1,000}{4}$$

$$= \$553$$

Sum of the Years' Digits

The other widely used method of accelerated depreciation can be illustrated simply with a relatively short life of four years:

$1 + 2 + 3 + 4 = 10$

Of the total amount to be depreciated, 4/10 would be charged off the
first year, 3/10 the second year, 2/10 the third, and the remaining 1/10 in
the last year.

For a ten-year life, the sum of the digits $(10 + 9 + 8$ etc.) would be 55,
and thus the depreciation schedule would be:

Depreciable Amount = \$11,000 cost − \$1,000 Salvage Value

Year	Fraction	Depreciation	Book Value at End of Period
1	10/55	\$1,818	\$9,182
2	9/55	1,636	7,546
3	8/55	1,455	6,091
4	7/55	1,273	4,818
5	6/55	1,091	3,727
6	5/55	909	2,818
7	4/55	727	2,091
8	3/55	545	1,546
9	2/55	364	1,182
10	1/55	182	1,000
		\$10,000	

(Note that salvage value must be taken into account in sum of the years'
digits depreciation.)

The following table compares the three methods of depreciation--
straight line, double declining balance and SYD (sum of the years'

70

digits)--with salvage value used in straight line and SYD:

	Annual Depreciation Expense			Closing Book Value		
Year	Straight Line	200% Decl. Bal.	SYD	Straight Line	200% Decl. Bal.	SYD
1	$1,000	$2,200	$1,818	$10,000	$9,800	$9,182
2	1,000	1,960	1,636	9,000	7,784	7,546
3	1,000	1,568	1,455	8,000	6,272	6,091
4	1,000	1,254	1,273	7,000	5,018	4,818
5	1,000	1,004	1,091	6,000	4,014	3,727
6	1,000	803	909	5,000	3,211	2,818
7	1,000	553*	727	4,000	2,658	2,091
8	1,000	553*	545	3,000	2,104	1,546
9	1,000	553*	364	2,000	1,553	1,182
10	1,000	553*	182	1,000	1,000	1,000

*Converted to the straight line method in year 7

There are a number of other highly specialized methods of depreciation, but in many cases they use sophisticated statistical techniques or are limited to certain industries where special conditions are found.

Declining balance and SYD, the two accelerated methods, both give recognition to the fact that the real depreciation in the asset's value is generally greater in the earlier years. And of course they have the added advantage of providing larger depreciation deductions and hence lower taxable income and lower income taxes in the early years.

Tax accounting vs. book accounting

Sometimes management may feel that accelerated depreciation charges the cost of the asset off too fast, with the result of making the income look too low. And yet they still want the tax benefits of using accelerated depreciation. This dilemma is resolved by keeping two sets of books. (Contrary to what some laymen may think, that is perfectly legal and proper; in fact, it is done by virtually every major company.)

In its tax returns the company uses the fastest possible depreciation that the IRS will allow, in order to reduce its taxes to the lowest permissible amount. But in financial reports to its stockholders and creditors, it takes depreciation at slower rates that it considers more realistic. This means that income taxes actually paid will be lower than if they were calculated on the basis of the stockholder reports.

Eventually, though, there will be a day of reckoning. In the later years, depreciation charges will be lower on the tax returns, and taxable income and taxes will be higher, than on the reports to stockholders. Thus, taxes are saved in the earlier years but must be paid in the later years.

In effect, a significant amount of income taxes has been postponed, or deferred. Thus, if the company keeps two sets of books, its stockholder reports will show a two-part income tax charge, consisting of taxes actually paid plus the taxes that are deferred as a result of accelerated depreciation. The deferred taxes charged to income are carried on the balance sheet as "deferred income taxes."* In effect, this is a reserve for the taxes that will have to be paid in future years.

Depletion

If the asset is a mineral reserve--such as coal or copper in the ground, or oil or natural gas--the same type of accounting is used, but it is called depletion rather than depreciation. Cost depletion is a method closely analagous to straight line depreciation. The cost of acquiring the mineral reserve, less residual value (equivalent to salvage value), is charged off uniformly over the estimated life of the reserve. After the

* This is the preferred and most conservative way to handle deferred taxes. Some industries use the "flow-through" method, in which the full tax benefit is reported as income. But that can be misleading since it does not give the analyst a warning that higher taxes will have to be paid in the future.

cost has been recovered, no additional depletion charges may be taken even though the mine or oil well may still be producing. Similarly, a machine may still be usable after it has been completely written off, but if the company continues to use it, no more depreciation can be deducted.

Another type of depletion is called percentage depletion, and this can continue long after the cost has been recovered if the mine or well is still producing. The company is allowed to charge off a fixed percentage of mineral revenues each year, without regard to the cost of the asset, as long as revenues continue. Percentage depletion is generally intended to provide an incentive to investing in mineral ventures that may have high risks, such as exploratory drilling for oil and gas. If the search is successful and the well produces oil or gas, percentage depletion provides a tax shelter for some of the income that the well produces. (But only for individuals, partnerships, and smaller oil companies; large companies are no longer allowed to take percentage depletion.)

Before leaving the subject of depreciation and depletion, it is important to correct one common misconception. Depreciation allowances and the depreciation reserve are sometimes considered to be money that is put aside to buy a new machine when the old one wears out. This is not an accurate statement of the purpose of depreciation. Rather, what depreciation does is to allocate the cost of an asset in a realistic way over the years of its use.

It can be readily seen that, in inflationary times such as the present, a depreciation reserve equal to 100% of the original cost of an item purchased years ago will fall far short of what will be needed to replace the asset.

Chapter Eight

CAPITALIZATION

We have seen that the capitalization or capital structure of a company includes debt that is owed and equity that is owned. However, current liabilities are not considered part of the long-term or permanent capital, since they will have to be repaid soon and thus represent money that is available to the company only for a short time.

Debt that doesn't have to be repaid within one year is considered to be part of the capital structure. (Capitalization and capital structure means the same thing. And another phrase--funds employed in the business-- is sometimes used, too, as on page 16.)

Long-term or permanent capital provides the funds that the company invests in its permanent assets, such as real estate, plant, and equipment. Capital is raised principally from the owners of the company and from lenders who are willing to wait for a number of years for repayment. But there are several different types of debt capital and also several types of equity capital.

The capitalization is essentially all on the right side of the balance sheet except current liabilities. In this chapter we will examine in more detail the accounting treatment of the various components of the capital structure. We shall see that, in addition to debt and equity, there are several hybrids that combine debt and equity. And there is one strange item that cannot really be classified as either, and yet it is a major component of the capital structure in many large companies. Thus, the four components are:

- Debt: Mortgage bonds and other secured debt; unsecured debt; leasing.

- Equity: Common stock; other types of equity securities.

- Hybrid: Preferred stock, or minority interest, or convertible securities.

- Unclassifiable: Deferred income taxes.

Mortgage bonds and other secured debt

Most families have a large long-term debt obligation--the mortgage secured by the house or condominium they live in. They have borrowed a large amount of money to buy their home and have pledged it as collateral for the loan, which they are repaying over an extended period, perhaps 20 years or more.

Many businesses do exactly the same thing. They negotiate long-term borrowings to buy or build the facilities and equipment that they will use permanently in the business--factory buildings, warehouses and retail stores, machinery and trucks, for example. The property and equipment is often pledged as security for the debt.

The borrower's burden

When a company starts out in business, it will probably have trouble borrowing money and will have to pledge its assets in order to do so. The same thing is true if it has a spotty profit record or a poor credit rating as a result of lateness in paying bills. The lender, because of his concern about the company's credit and ability to repay, wants the comfort and security that is provided by a pledge of fixed assets. If the company got into real trouble the lender could foreclose and take possession of the assets and sell them to recoup what he is owed. Some lenders will lend against a pledge of inventory and accounts receivable; this is called commercial financing or factoring, and it is essentially short-term financing. It should not be used to raise permanent capital, although some companies use it that way because they are unable to raise long-term capital on terms that they consider acceptable.

Unsecured long-term debt

Fifty years ago lenders always required a pledge of assets as security. Unsecured debt was virtually unheard of. But gradually this began to change, especially for companies that were well established and had long records of continuing profitability and strong balance sheets. Lenders came to understand that the real security for their loan was the strength of the company and its ability to continue to earn profits, rather than the fixed assets. Indeed, it often happened that if the company could not earn a profit, its fixed assets weren't worth much, either. (Holders of mortgage

76

bonds of the Penn Central and other bankrupt railroads found this out to their sorrow.)

As a result, strong and well-established companies rarely have to pledge their assets in order to borrow. They usually borrow on an unsecured basis, sometimes for as long as 30 or 35 years. They give the lender a promissory note, which may be called exactly that--a note. It may also be called a bond or a loan. Another common term is debenture--a debenture is simply an unsecured note or bond repayable in more than one year.

Terms of long-term debt

There is a ranking among creditors (and owners, too); some have priority over others. The holders of the mortgage debt have the strongest (most senior) claim, since certain assets have been pledged to secure their claim. Other senior or first-priority creditors are banks, trade creditors, and holders of bonds or notes that are designated as senior. Although they don't have a lien on any particular asset, they have first claim on the general assets of the company.

Sometimes a company will issue junior or subordinated debt, which is in a secondary position. If the company goes bankrupt, the senior lenders and creditors are supposed to be paid in full before the subordinated lenders (or any of the owners) get anything. Some companies even have three levels of debt: senior, subordinated, and junior subordinated. This is common among large finance companies, which do a great deal of borrowing and have large and complicated capital structures.

Long-term bonds or notes, whether secured or unsecured, are repayable at maturity, which may be five or seven years from the date of borrowing. Or it may be much longer, as long as 35 or even 40 years in the case of publicly offered bonds of large companies with strong credit.

Waiting for the balloon to go up

However, there is almost always an installment repayment schedule that requires that a large percentage of the debt be paid before maturity. The installments may or may not be uniform as they are with most home mortgages. For example, a 10-year note might be repaid on a schedule something like this:

Year 1   -   Interest only.

Year 2   -   Interest only.

Years 3-9 -   10 percent of principal per year in quarterly installments of 2½ percent each.

Year 10   -   Three quarterly installments of 2½ percent each with a final payment of 22½ percent at the end of the year, which is the final maturity date.

This large final payment is known as a balloon.

Covenants

Debentures and other long-term unsecured borrowings usually have a number of contractual promises by the borrower contained in the note or debt instruments. These are called covenants.

One of the most important covenants is called a negative pledge cause. This provision says, in effect: "I won't pledge my assets to you (lender), but as long as I owe you this money I agree that I won't pledge them to anybody else either."

78

Another frequently used covenant is a limitation on common dividends. The note agreement may specify that dividends on common stock (together with amounts spent to purchase or redeem stock) will not exceed current earnings, or perhaps that they may not exceed some percentage (less than 100 percent) of earnings.

The note may require the borrowing company to maintain working capital at or above a certain dollar figure, or it may specify that the borrower agrees that the ratio of current assets to current liabilities will be kept at or above a certain level.

The note agreement normally provides that a violation of any covenant would put the loan immediately into default, which would mean that it must be repaid in full immediately.

Bond prices and values stated on the balance sheet

When a loan is negotiated with a single lender or a small number of lenders, a note agreement, or indenture, will be signed. The agreement is a long promissory note containing several pages of covenants, terms, and conditions. When bonds are sold at a public offering, the covenants and terms are set forth in the prospectus.

In either case the company may receive slightly less or slightly more than the stated value or par value of the note or the bonds. The $1,000 bond may be sold for $996 or for $1,004. And sometimes the discount or premium is considerably greater.*

If the bonds are sold at a premium, that means that the company re-

* A well-known example of a discount bond is the Series E savings bond. A $50 bond is sold for $37.50 and a $100 bond for $75. However, Series E bonds are unusual in that the increase from the purchase price to the face value constitutes interest. By contrast, interest on corporate bonds is generally paid directly to the bondholder every six months.

ceived more than it will pay back when the bonds mature. Alternatively, if the bonds are sold at a discount, the company receives less than it will eventually pay back.

Bond premium is entered on the balance sheet as a liability. Bond discount, and also the expenses of selling the issue (such as legal, printing, SEC, and underwriting fees) are entered as an asset on the balance sheet. As the bonds are retired, the premium will be taken into income as a nonoperating income item and the discount will be deducted as a nonoperating expense.

Leasing

A technique that closely resembles secured long-term borrowing is the rental of the capital equipment that the business needs from the owner, which may be a leasing company. In some cases a long-term equipment lease is virtually indistinguishable from an installment purchase. The leasing company, or seller, retains title to the asset in one case and a lien on the asset in the other. If the lease agreement gives the renter an opportunity to buy the asset at the end of the lease term for a nominal sum, then the lease is simply a disguised installment purchase.

Accounting controversies

The similarity between the two types of financing gave rise to two major accounting controversies in the 1960s and the 1970s. One problem with leasing was that lenders and creditors felt that a company's balance sheet looked stronger than it really was if the company rented, rather than bought, large amounts of property.

80

The firm would have sizable future commitments to pay rentals. Although these commitments did not appear on the balance sheet, they represented a major obligation, since the company could not continue to operate if it failed to pay the rent on its essential capital assets.

The accounting rules have now been changed as a result of this concern and of the enormous growth of leasing. In general, long-term leases are now required to be carried on the balance sheet as long-term debt, which is what they really are in most cases.

The second controversy about the lease accounting concerned the tax treatment of the rental payments. In some cases, the monthly rent was approximately equal to what the monthly installment payment would have been on a purchase. If the lease was really a disguised installment purchase, the IRS was very unhappy about the arrangement, since the equipment user could deduct the entire rental payment as a business expense. By contrast, an installment purchaser could deduct only the interest, not the portion of the payment representing the principal. As a result, the IRS established some detailed requirements that must be met if the transaction is to be treated as a lease for tax purposes.

Equity capital

The cash invested in the business or the property contributed by the owners is the equity part of the capital structure. Owners normally invest cash or property when the company is organized and starts its business. They may make additional contributions later. The later contributions may be additional amounts paid into the company treasury for new shares of stock purchased by investors, or they may be in the form of earnings retained by the company rather than paid out as dividends.

Common stock is frequently sold at prices in excess of par value. For example, stock with a par value of $1 per share might be sold at $10 per share. In this case, the $1 would be entered on the balance sheet as common stock and the $9 as additional paid-in capital or capital surplus. As the company earned profits, they would be credited to retained earnings. If dividends were paid, retained earnings would be reduced accordingly. If dividends exceed retained earnings, the excess is deducted from either paid-in capital or the common stock account, and such dividends are considered return of capital rather than ordinary income to the stockholders.

Thus the equity portion of the balance sheet usually consists of at least three items--common stock, paid-in capital, and retained earnings. (The total of these three items is sometimes reduced by treasury stock-- stock that the company has redeemed or repurchased and is holding in the treasury.)

The total equity figure is a very important one to both stockholders and creditors. The components of the total have little significance. The par or stated value is unimportant, and the price paid by the investors is important only at the time of the transaction. As time passes it will have less significance and within a few years none at all (except that it is the cost basis of the investor's holding, to be used in determining capital gain or loss for tax purposes when he sells, and also in determining the company's return on invested capital). The market price, if the stock is traded, will be determined primarily by the total equity (including retained earnings) and by the company's current results and its prospects. The value of the company's stock, if it were liquidated, could be more or

82

less than the market value of its stock, depending on what could be realized from the sale of its assets.

Let us examine a sequence of equity transactions as they would be shown on the balance sheet. Assume that:

• A company is organized in December 1960 and sells 10,000 shares of $1 par stock for $10 per share.

• In 1961 it incurs a loss of $25,000.

• In 1962 it makes a profit after taxes of $40,000.

• In the years 1963-69 it makes profits after taxes totaling $500,000, and in 1969 it splits its stock 100 for 1, reducing the par value to 1¢ per share.

• In 1970 it sells 200,000 new shares for $8 per share. It breaks even for the year, showing neither profit nor loss.

• In 1979-79 it earns $2,400,000 after taxes.

Balance sheet items at year-end

	1960	1961	1962	1969	1970	1979
Common stock	$10,000	$10,000	$10,000	$10,000	$12,000	$12,000
Additional paid-in earnings	90,000	90,000	90,000	90,000	1,688,000	1,688,000
Retained earnings	0	(25,000)	15,000	515,000	515,000	2,915,000
TOTAL COMMON EQUITY	$100,000	$75,000	$115,000	$615,000	$2,215,000	$4,615,000
Number of common shares	10,000	10,000	10,000	1,000,000	1,200,000	1,200,000
Book value per share	$10.00	$ 7.50	$11.50	61½¢	$ 1.845	$ 3.845

In this example, the company did not pay any dividends. All of the proceeds from sales of stock and also the earnings were retained. Note that the stock split did not constitute a dividend; no cash was paid to the stockholders and there was no change in the equity entries on the balance sheet.

If the company had paid a stock dividend, as some companies do, it would not change the total equity figure either or result in a taxable dividend to stockholders. It would, however, result in a transfer from retained earnings to paid-in capital.

It should be noted that the figures on the balance sheet would not be affected by transfers of stock from one stockholder to another at whatever price they agreed upon. The payment would be made by the buyer to the seller and the company would not receive any part of it.

Shares of stock can be compared to automobiles in this regard. General Motors builds a Chevrolet and sells it to the first purchaser and receives the purchase price. The car may be sold and resold many times as a used car, but GM is not involved in any of those transactions. Similarly, when a share of stock is originally issued by the company and sold to the first purchaser, the company receives the proceeds of the sale. The stock may be sold and resold many times thereafter, but the company is not involved in any of the sales after the first one. It cannot control the price of the shares or who the purchaser is, and of course it does not receive the proceeds of the sale.

Preferred stock—a debt-equity hybrid

The essential characteristic of equity investment is unlimited participation in growth, profit, and dividends. The owner or stockholder takes a risk by making an equity investment. He expects to be rewarded for taking the risk by dividends and capital gains if the company is successful. By contrast, the lender takes a lesser risk in most cases, and his reward is to get his money back with interest at a rate that was fixed at the time he made the loan. And generally that is all that he gets.

A preferred stock is considered in law and accounting to be a form of equity, but it really has more of the characteristics of debt. It is normally a fixed dollar obligation, which means that the preferred stockholder, like the lender, will eventually get back exactly the same number of dollars he originally invested, plus dividends at a predetermined rate. No matter how much profit the company makes, the preferred stockholder, like the lender, gets nothing extra.

Preferred stock ranks senior to common stock but junior to all creditors. Common stockholders cannot receive any dividends until all required preferred dividends have been paid. If the company loses money for a year or two, it may stop paying preferred dividends in order to conserve cash. Indeed, it may sometimes be required to suspend dividends by covenants in its long-term borrowing agreements. The preferred dividend requirement is almost always cumulative, which means that if preferred dividends are suspended for a time, all the back dividends (called dividends in arrears) must be paid in full before the company may pay any common dividends.

The rights of the preferred

Preferred stockholders usually have voting rights along with common stockholders in the annual election of directors and in other matters. However, it frequently happens that the common stockholders have far more shares--and votes--with the result that the holders of preferred stock may not have an effective means of asserting their rights and views in opposition to those of the common stockholders. To remedy this, the corporate charter may provide that, if preferred dividends are suspended, the preferred stockholders as a group have the right to elect a majority of the board of directors.

If the company should be liquidated, either voluntarily or in bankruptcy, the preferred stock is entitled to be paid off at par or stated value--if there are sufficient assets remaining after paying the creditors--before the common stockholders get anything.

In years past, preferred stock normally had no fixed maturity or redemption requirement. Once issued it would usually be outstanding forever, like the common stock, unless the company chose to repurchase or redeem it voluntarily. Now, however, the custom is to have a sinking fund, which is a requirement that the company redeem the issue in installments. A typical sinking fund provision might require that, beginning with the tenth year after the stock is issued, the company must redeem 10 percent of the issue each year. This would mean that all of the stock would be redeemed within 20 years.

Preferred stocks are now rather rare. They are still issued by utilities, finance companies, and others with large capital needs and elaborate and complex capital structures, but most managements will avoid issuing preferred stock if they possibly can. The reason is simple: dividends on preferred stock are not deductible as a business expense. Since interest is deductible, management would rather borrow than sell preferred stock if it can.

Other types of equity securities

Despite the decline of preferred stock, some companies use something similar when they create two classes of common stock. For example, there might be a Class A common and a Class B common. A typical provision might be that the Class A stock has a dividend preference up to $1 per year per share of Class A, and that any additional dividends would be paid equally to Class A and Class B. The Class A stock might also have a preference in the event the company is liquidated.

Options and warrants are another type of equity security--perhaps quasi-security would be a more accurate way to describe them. They are contracts entitling the holder to buy common stock at a fixed price for a fixed period of time; for example, at $4 per share until December 31, 1982. (Options and warrants are essentially the same, but warrants usually run for several years and options are often good for only a few months.)

Holders of options and warrants have no ownership interest or dividend or any other rights until they exercise the option or warrant and buy the stock. After that, the option or warrant is canceled and the holder is in the same position as any other stockholder.

Some options are sold by the company directly, but a number of options are created by securities dealers and traded on stock exchanges without any control or participation by the company itself.

Minority interest

Some balance sheets carry an item called minority interest just below the liabilities but above the equity entries. Minority interest is created in a merger and consolidation.

When Company A acquires Company B, it normally combines all of the assets, liabilities, sales, expenses, and profits, after eliminating any items that reflect transactions between the two companies. The result is a series of consolidated financial statements reflecting the new and larger company. The separate identities of Company A and Company B are submerged in the consolidated statement and it is no longer possible to identify separate financial items of A and B.

However, it sometimes happens that A acquires a majority of the stock and control of B but that some of the B shareholders keep their stock and refused to sell it to A. In this case, Company A must continue to keep separate Company B books and accounts, although it does not necessarily publish them, and it must continue to respect the rights and privileges of the minority stockholders of Company B. Thus, even though the minority interest represents common stock, it has a claim on the assets and earnings of Company B that is senior to the claim of the Company A stockholders. Although it is equity, it is also something like a liabilitity, since the combined company "owes" something to the holders of the minority interest.

Convertible securities

A convertible debenture is a debt obligation that may be converted into equity at the option of the holder. For example, the debenture might be convertible at the rate of $25 per share, which means that each $1,000 debenture could be converted into 40 shares of common stock. Convertible debentures are generally subordinated to other long-term debt and to senior creditors.

A preferred stock may also be convertible into common stock.

The conversion privilege is available only once, and it is a one-way street: that is, the bondholder may, at his option, exchange his debenture for common stock, but then the debenture is canceled and he is in the same position as any other common stockholder. He has no right to convert back to the debenture.

Although the conversion normally takes place only at the bondholder's (or preferred stockholder's) option, the company may in some cases be able to force the conversion. For example, suppose the bond is convertible at $25 but the market price of the common stock is $50 per share. That means the debenture is worth 200 percent of par value, since the $1,000 debenture can be converted into 40 shares of stock that could be sold for $2,000. The company may announce that in 30 days it will call or redeem the debentures at, say, 107 percent of par value. (Its right to redeem the debentures at its option was spelled out at the time the bonds were issued.) Practically all holders of the convertible debenture, except those who don't read or understand their mail, will convert before deadline so as to realize the $2,000 value rather than selling the bond back to the company for $1,070.

Deferred income taxes

This is another hybrid item that appears on many balance sheets (pages 71-72). It certainly isn't equity, and it is an obligation that will probably have to be paid someday. But it isn't exactly debt, either, since the government does not have a present claim for any additional taxes. If the company should liquidate, the deferred taxes may never have to be paid by the company, although the stockholders on liquidation might pay additional taxes to the extent that the company had taken accelerated depreciation on assets.

Chapter Nine

COST ACCOUNTING
AND COST CONTROL

One of the most important problems that faces a business manager is keeping costs under control. And the manager cannot even begin the cost control effort unless he receives reports showing a detailed breakdown of the costs and expenses incurred in operating the business. The reports should be as current as possible. It is essential to identify as early as possible those costs which are getting out of hand so that corrective action can be taken without delay.

Thus one of the major functions of the bookkeeping and accounting process is to develop accurate reports of costs which have been prepared and presented so as to call attention to those costs that are running higher than forecast. These reports should also clearly pinpoint the amount of the variance between actual costs and those costs allowed for in the budget.

A full spectrum of costs

Originally, cost accounting dealt only with costs of manufacturing and production. But accounting today analyzes all of the costs of doing business. Accounting reports cover other costs of operation, including costs in such diverse areas as office management, personnel replacement, and the efficiency of the company's sales staff--as well as the traditional production costs.

The data prepared by cost accountants not only provide detailed information on current operations, but also present an excellent base for future planning. The cost accounting may show management, for example, that it is unprofitable to process a sales order smaller than a certain dollar amount. Or it may point up the fact that an outside vendor or contractor might perform a particular service function at a lower cost than can be met by doing it internally.

Direct and indirect costs

The distinction between direct and indirect costs is an essential part of cost accounting. Direct costs are those that can be readily identified with each unit of production. Indirect costs are those that cannot be so identified.

For example, the cost of raw material used in production is a direct cost. Suppose a certain type of steel costs $400 per ton, or 20 cents per pound, and that each unit of a particular manufactured item contains half a pound of steel. Also suppose that metal loss through shrinkage and scrap generally averages five percent over a period of time. The steel cost of this particular product, therefore, would be clearly identifiable at $10\frac{1}{2}$

cents per unit produced.

Factory labor is another direct cost. Suppose that a production worker performs a machining operation on this product, and that is his only job. He machines approximately 160 units in an eight-hour day, or an average of 20 per hour. His wage is $11.00 per hour, consisting of $8.80 in direct pay and $2.20 per hour for Social Security, medical insurance, the pension plan, holidays and vacations, and other fringe benefits. The cost of this worker is readily identified as 50 cents per unit of this product, since he doesn't work on anything else.

By contrast, consider the salary of the factory bookkeeper who collects time cards, totals up hours worked, and forwards the information to the company payroll department. Or the cost of the security service that provides guards when the plant is closed. These are production costs, since they are necessary in connection with the operation of the plant. But they cannot be readily identified with units of production, and thus they are indirect costs.

The general overhead of the company, including most executive salaries and such items as the cost of occupancy of the headquarters building, consists almost entirely of indirect costs. Accountants sometimes refer to overhead and other indirect costs as "the burden."

Contribution accounting

A useful cost analysis can be developed by isolating the direct costs for each product or product line to determine the contribution made by that product toward carrying the burden of the company's overhead. A contribution statement shows direct costs only:

92

PRODUCT X

Contribution Analysis

			Per Unit
Net Sales			$10.00
Direct costs:			
Raw materials	$2.50		
Direct labor	4.00		
Supplies	.50		
Direct manufacturing costs		$7.00	
Direct selling costs		.50	
Total direct costs			7.50
Contribution			$ 2.50

A series of contribution statements for each product will show how much each is contributing to the payment of overhead. In addition, it highlights the most profitable products, which products are carrying more of their share, and which products management may decide to promote more aggressively. It may also show that certain other products are making a very small contribution, or perhaps none at all, and might appropriately be discontinued.

The contribution analysis is a good example of how cost accounting techniques are used as a management tool that provides information on which decisions can be based. This information is for use within the company only. It is not intended for publication or for use in preparing the corporate tax returns.

Variable vs. fixed costs

Another essential principle of cost accounting is the distinction between variable and fixed costs. Variable costs are those that change in a direct relationship to the volume of production, such as raw materials or factory labor.

Fixed costs are those that do not vary with volume. Examples of fixed costs are liability insurance, real estate taxes, legal fees, and most executive salaries.

There is also a hybrid category of costs that are semifixed and semivariable. They might be fixed within a certain range of production or volume but might then increase to a higher level when production rises above that range.

For example, factory supervision would be a fixed cost as long as the plant operated on one shift. But if the need for increased production required a second shift to be added, it would be necessary to hire a number of new foremen and supervisors. Thus supervisory costs would increase sharply with the addition of the second shift and then remain at the new level, without variation for changes in the rate of production of either the first or the second shift.

The classification of variable and fixed costs is similar to that of direct costs--similar but not identical. That is, direct costs are generally variable, but not always. Indirect costs are generally fixed, but not always.

For example, consider a plant that produces only a single product. The occupancy cost* of the building is a direct cost in this case, since it is clearly identifiable with that particular product. But it is a fixed cost, not a variable cost. It amounts to roughly the same figure every month, irrespective of the number of units produced in the plant. Indeed,

---

*The occupancy cost is the rent on a rented building and ownership costs of an owned building, such as real estate taxes, mortgage insurance, and depreciation. It also includes maintenance, fire insurance, guard service, and other items.

it probably would not change significantly in most cases even if the plant produced nothing at all, as might be the case if the plant was closed, say, by a strike.

Cost accounting systems

Job order cost accounting is used where each unit of production and the direct costs connected with it can be readily identified. This method would be used by a builder completing a dozen houses or two office buildings, or by a construction contractor building a dam in Africa and a generating plant in Missouri.

The alternative approach is process cost accounting, which is typically used by manufacturers with a large number of product lines, so that costing by individual unit is difficult or impossible.

Standard costs

Cost accountants normally develop standard costs for each product. Standard costs are arrived at after an extensive analytical study of information obtained from the engineering, purchasing, and personnel staffs and others who can contribute information on what costs should be for the particular product.

Thus, standard costs represent a goal, but if the analytical work is done properly it will allow a margin for error. As a result, the goal will be a realizable one, rather than an ideal situation that is unattainable in the real world.

All items affecting the cost of a product should be included in the standard cost analysis. Here is an example:

STANDARD COST SHEET

PRODUCT A
DECEMBER 31, 1980   unit = 8.0 kilos

Raw materials	Kilograms/Unit	$/Kilo	Total/Unit
Material A	1.0	$ 0.30	$0.300
Material B	2.0	0.45	0.900
Material C	5.0	0.50	2.500
Total	5.0	0.50	$3.700
Shrinkage 5%			.185
Total raw material cost			$3.885

	Amount/Unit	$/Carton	
Packaging material			
Carton	1.00	.75	$0.750

	Hours/Unit	$/Hour	
Direct labor			
Mixing	0.10	8.00	$ .800
Packaging	0.05	10.00	.500
Total direct labor			$1.300
Total			$5.935
Rejects 3%			.162
Total cost/unit			$6.097

Standard costs are a goal or a norm for operations, and the next step is to analyze actual costs to determine how much they vary from these standards. If the price of material A for the period is actually $.320/kilo, there would be an unfavorable raw material cost variance of $.020 per unit.

Standard costs are not necessarily the same as budgeted costs. They should be the same under ideal conditions, but there may be occasional unusual circumstances in which it is known that standard costs cannot be achieved, and so the budget anticipates the variance from standard. For example, when a new product line is started or a new plant is opened, it is normal to expect some bugs and inefficiencies that will take time to work out. The budget would take these normal start-up problems into account.

Standard costs are absolutely crucial in new product decisions, when management has to decide "go or no go." The decision to go ahead, if it is made, will be based on a belief that a satisfactory sales volume can be developed at a selling price that provides a good margin of profit over cost. If the costs as projected are too low, then the product cannot achieve the desired level of profitability.

Variance analysis

The books of account show standard costs, which represent the goal or the desired norm, and also variances, which are the differences between actual costs and standard costs.

The inclusion of standard costs in the books of account is an unusual exception to the rule that only actual figures and not theoretical ones are used. But they are extremely useful in providing a target or an objective for management to try to reach.

The reports identify each variance, thus providing management with information as to where the problems and inefficiencies are.

We have focused on costs in this discussion, and indeed a large share of management attention is directed toward cost variances. But there are also variances in other items, such as sales and production.

Variances are usually bad news--whether they be costs higher than standard or sales below budget--but of course sometimes there is good news, too. For example:

	Actual	Budget	Variance
Net sales	$100,000	$70,000	$30,000
Unit sales	12,500	10,000	2,500
Unit price	8.00	7.00	1.00

In this situation the total $30,000 variance consists of two components.

Since 12,500 units were sold at $1 per unit higher than budget, $12,500 of the variance resulted from the higher selling price. The rest of the variance--$17,500--was attributable to increased volume (2,500 unit sales variance multiplied by the $7.00 budgeted selling price).

Variance analysis can be applied to any of the elements of the operation of the business--number of employees, product mix, advertising expenditures, hours worked, and so on. Here is an illustration of a variance analysis of direct labor costs:

	Actual	Standard	Variance
Total direct labor costs	$6,500	$4,590	+$1,910
Hours, regular	1,100	1,000	+ 100
Hours, overtime	100	10	+ 90
Rate/hour, regular	5.00	4.50	+ .50
Rate/hour, overtime	10.00	9.00	+ 1.00

Variance due to hours, regular 100 hours x $4.50/hour	+$ 450
Variance due to rate/hour, regular 1,100 hours x $.50/hour	+ 550
Total variance, regular time labor	+$1,000
Variance due to hours, overtime 90 hours x $9.00/hour	+ 810
Variance due to rate/hour, overtime 100 hours x $1.00/hour	+ 100
Total variance, overtime labor	+$ 910
Total variance, direct labor	+$1,910

Break-even analysis

In making a decision whether to go ahead with a proposed new product, management should estimate the level of expected profits at various levels of sales and various selling prices. It asks the cost accountant: If we set the selling price at X, how many units will we have to sell to break even? And how much profit will we make if we sell 20 percent more than that? 50 percent more? 100 percent more?

The same type of analysis is used in setting the price of a new product or in deciding whether to change the price of an existing product. If we lower the price, it will make the product easier to sell, but how many more units will we have to sell to earn the same profits? Or--if customer attitudes seem favorable--management may consider raising prices. Then: How much more profit will we make if we can hold unit sales steady at the higher price? And: What will profits be at the higher price if unit sales decline by five percent? 10 percent? 30 percent?

Break-even analysis focuses on the essential fact that fixed costs per unit decline as volume increases. Thus the separation of fixed costs from variable costs is the first step in break-even analysis, as in this illustration:

PRODUCT Y COST DATA

Fixed costs	Amount
Real estate taxes	$10,000
Supervisory labor & administration	3,000
Insurance	2,000
Other	5,000
Total fixed costs	$20,000

Variable costs	$/Unit
Direct labor	$ 1.50
Raw materials	3.00
Supplies	.50
Total manufacturing	$ 5.00
Selling commission	1.00
Variable cost per unit	$ 6.00

Selling price	$10.00 per unit

To determine the break-even volume--the level of sales and production at which revenue would be exactly equal to the total of fixed and var iable costs--this formula is used:

$$\text{Break-even volume} = \frac{\text{Total fixed costs}}{\text{Selling price} - \text{variable costs}}$$

$$\text{Break-even volume} = \frac{\$20{,}000}{(\$10.00 - \$6.00)} = 5{,}000 \text{ units}$$

It is useful to present break-even data in the form of a graph in order to highlight the different levels of profitability at various rates of sales. Also, a variety of possible selling prices can be considered. (See page 102 for a break-even graph.)

Direct costing

Direct costing is an accounting technique that provides cost data that are not distorted by the effect of changes in the volume of production.

By way of background, a conventional accounting system enters costs in inventory on a per unit basis. Budgeted manufacturing costs for the year are divided by expected unit volume; the result is budgeted unit cost. In months when the production volume exceeds budget, the excess is known as over-absorbed burden and deferred to a future period. If this happens for an extended period, the budget should be adjusted.

Similarly, if costs are over budget for an extended period, it may be necessary at the end of the year to absorb a large expense item, since the unit cost was set too low during the year.

By contrast, the direct costing method excludes indirect costs in order to focus attention on direct costs.

Here is a comparison of the two systems:

100

Assumptions

	Period I	Period II
Actual production	8,000 units	2,000 units
Budgeted production	5,000 units	5,000 units
Sales volume	5,000 units	5,000 units
Inventory	3,000 units	0 units

Sales Price $10/unit
Direct manufacturing costs $3/unit
Indirect manufacturing costs $4/unit $20,000/period
Selling and administrative costs $2,500/period

Statement of Income and Expenses

	Period I		Period II	
	Conventional	Direct	Conventional	Direct
Gross sales	$50,000	$50,000	$ 5,000	$ 5,000
Cost of goods sold				
Opening inventory	0	0	21,000	9,000
Cost of manufactured goods	56,000	$24,000	14,000	6,000
Closing inventory	21,000	9,000	0	0
Cost of goods sold	35,000	15,000	35,000	15,000
Gross profit	15,000	35,000	15,000	35,000
Selling, admin. expenses	2,500	2,500	2,500	2,500
(Over)Underabsorbed burden	(12,000)	--	12,000	--
Indirect mfg. expenses	--	20,000	--	20,000
Net operating income	$ 500	$12,500	$24,500	$12,500

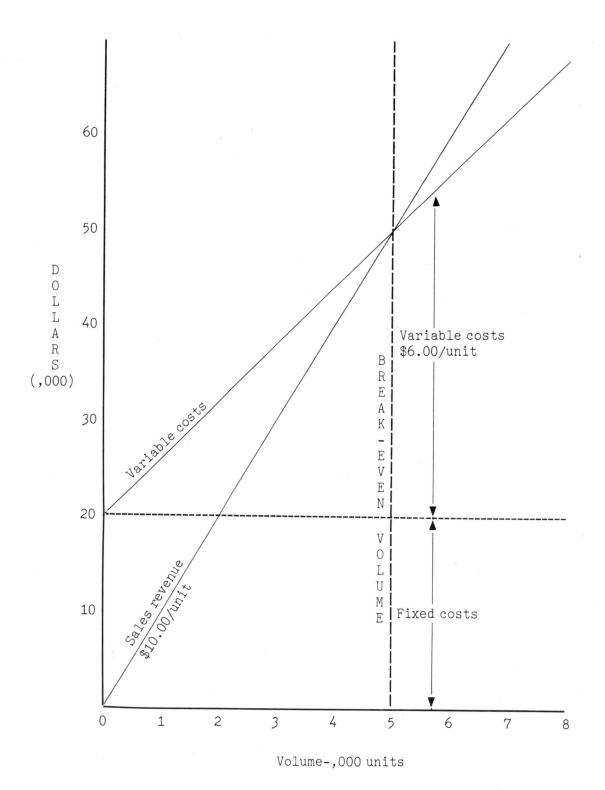

Volume-,000 units

Chapter Ten

INTERNAL MANAGEMENT: ACCOUNTING, BUDGETING, AND PLANNING

One of the most important objectives of the bookkeeping and accounting system is to inform management about what has happened financially-- what revenues have been received and what expenses have been incurred. The financial statements are essentially historical; that is, they reflect the past. But they are also an essential tool in planning for the future.

In this chapter we will explore the various ways in which the accounting system assists management in monitoring and assigning responsibility for what has happened in the past and in budgeting, planning, and making decisions about the future.

Responsibility accounting

In a conventional accounting system, costs and expenses are normally broken down according to the product or department that receives the bene-

103

fit. For example, the personnel and other costs of the typing pool and the in-house print shop are allocated to those executives and departments who use their services. The allocation is most logical if it is based on use of the services, but it may also be made according to dollar investment, ability to pay, or any other formula or rationale that management considers appropriate.

The result is that a department head may find that a significant part of the costs allocated to his department are not within his control. They may increase as a result of inefficiencies in the operation of another department, or because of a management decision, sometimes a rather arbitrary one, as to how costs of another department are allocated.

By contrast, responsibility accounting requires that each manager be charged for all costs over which he has direct control, but not for any others. Thus there is no internal reallocation of costs. Responsibility accounting produces a flow of reports that match the company's organization chart.

Costs are allocated to those departments that control them. And they are broken down between fixed and variable costs (page 93). At the end of each accounting period each department prepares a report showing actual costs, the variances from budgeted costs, and the reason for the variances. These reports are transmitted to the next higher level of the organization, consolidated with others, and then forwarded higher still. Eventually top management receives a companywide report that shows costs and variances and enables it to identify the manager who is responsible for each variance.

Responsibility accounting helps management to locate problems and to take corrective action rapidly, and also, of course, to identify those operations which are being run efficiently and to reward those responsible for so running them.

The reports produced under responsibility accounting are valid only for internal purposes. They do not include overhead or profits; thus they show only part of the cost of that particular department or product. It would be very dangerous, for example, to use such a partial cost figure as a basis for setting a selling price.

Budgeting

A well-managed company must have a carefully prepared budget. The budget serves two functions, both absolutely essential. One purpose of the budget is to monitor current operations. Thus a control budget is prepared and used to detect problems through variance analysis. The other function of the budget is to facilitate planning for the future. Planning budgets may cover a period of a year, two years, five years, or even longer.*

Budget standards

Budgets must be prepared with meticulous care if they are to be sufficiently accurate to serve the desired purposes. The essential requirement for successful budgeting is to consider all of the consequences, both major and minor, of any anticipated change. For example, suppose the company projects a substantial increase in unit sales in the coming year. That will

*Some companies talk about using budgets in a third way, as a motivational tool. For example, the sales manager may think that the company can sell 10,000 units, but he prepares a budget projecting sales of 12,000 as a goad and an incentive to his salespeople. This motivational document should more properly be called a target rather than a budget.

require a proportionate increase in the cost of goods sold. Unless the inventory turnover can be materially speeded up, which is unlikely, the company will have to maintain substantially higher inventories. This, in turn, will mean a need for increased working capital, and perhaps bank borrowings, to carry the higher inventory. Additional warehouse space may be needed, as well.

In preparing budgets, the accounting staff must use the same accounting principles, the same cost categories, and in general exactly the same standards, methods, and procedures as are used in preparing the financial statements. Otherwise the variance analysis will be meaningless. Or misleading, which is worse.

Types of control budgets

A budget that will be used to control and evaluate current operations is usually a composite of a number of subsidiary budgets, combined into a unified system. The final budget will include:

• A cash budget reflecting estimates of what the company's cash position will be at various times during the period. When management sees the low point that the cash position will reach during the period, it may decide it is time to begin discussions of bank borrowing or some other type of financing.

• An inventory budget showing the amount of raw materials and components that must be purchased and the levels of inventory that must be maintained in order to have a sufficient supply of product on hand to meet the sales projections.

• A profit and loss budget.

• A capital expenditure budget, projecting the funds that will be needed to meet the company's long-term needs for plant and equipment.

These and other subsidiary budgets can be combined into a balance sheet budget and a sources and uses of funds budget. Since the latter would include an income statement budget as one of its components, the result would be a complete accounting system describing the total financial operations of the company.

Both the subsidiary budgets and the main budgets would then be used on an ongoing basis during the accounting period for variance analysis, which is the most basic accounting tool used by management to monitor and control operations.

Planning budgets

A planning budget may cover one year or a number of years in the future. A company might, for example, make sales projections for ten years ahead. The projections might be based on a variety of assumptions about the company's own operations and also about business conditions and the economy in general. A number of different budgets might be prepared; for example, one that assumed a recession and one that did not. Or three different budgets reflecting sales forecasts that are optimistic, pessimistic, and in between.

The planning budgets might show that a large number of new sales-people will have to be hired and trained, so the company might decide to establish a formal sales training program or plan to expand an existing one. Or the budgets might show that the company will need a new plant, with the result that it can begin immediately to study the location, size, cost, and so on. Planning and building the plant will require a number of years; the planning budget can alert management well ahead of time to the need to start preparations far enough in advance.

Flexible budgeting

Most budgets are based on a single projection of sales volume. But we have seen that in planning for a number of years ahead, it is sometimes wise to prepare a number of budgets representing varying degrees of optimism and various assumptions. Flexible budgeting is sometimes desirable in control budgets, too.

Flexible budgeting highlights the distinction between fixed and variable costs. For example, suppose that a company estimates that it can sell 50,000 units in the coming year. But it also thinks there is a possibility that business might improve significantly and it might sell 60,000 units. That will not require a new plant or a second shift; thus, fixed costs will be the same at both levels of production.

Here is a flexible budget that shows the two levels of production and sales:

	$/Unit	50,000 Units	60,000 Units
Fixed Costs			
Rent		$ 12,000	$ 12,000
Supervisory Salaries, Fixed Benefits		100,000	100,000
Insurance & Other Fixed Costs		25,000	25,000
Total Fixed Costs		$137,000	$137,000
Variable Costs			
Raw Materials	.25	$ 12,500	$ 15,000
Direct Labor	.75	37,000	45,000
Power	.10	5,000	6,000
Other Variable Costs	.20	10,000	12,000
Total Variable Costs		$ 65,000	$ 78,000
Total Plant Expense Budget		$192,000	$215,000

In flexible budgeting, fixed costs must be analyzed very carefully. They sometimes increase in a stair-step pattern, so that a small increase in volume may produce a sizable increase in fixed costs.

This is illustrated in the diagram below. Point B is the highest level of production that can be reached on one shift. Thus, a relatively small production increase, from B to C, will require adding a second shift; it will be a much more serious management decision with more important consequences than the larger production increase from point A to point B.

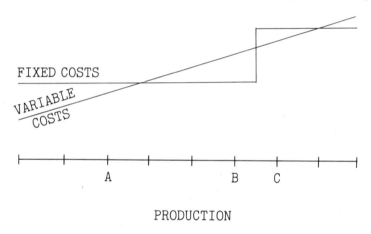

Zero-based budgeting

In conventional budgeting, it is generally assumed that each overhead department will receive a certain percentage increase over the previous year. If expenses are inflating at the rate of 10 percent a year, then each department head would expect at least a 10 percent increase. That would be considered an unchanged budget, and anything less would be considered a cut. The need for the department, its basic usefulness, is assumed and not questioned.

By contrast, a zero-based budgeting system does not assume anything. Its approach is: Let's go back to zero. Do we need this department? If it didn't exist, would we set it up? If we decide to do so, how much would we spend for it?

Each department is required to support its budget request with a decision package justifying its activities and listing various levels of operation, with a cost factor applied to each incremental level. Management reviews the budget and determines the level of priority for each alternative.

When all departments have submitted their reports and the total company budget is assembled, management determines the cutoff point in the scale of priorities. Everything above that point is funded; everything below it is cut off.

The advantage of zero-based budgeting is that it questions everything and assumes nothing. It does not allow old projects to be refunded and continued just because they are there. New projects can compete for funds on merit and have less inertia to overcome.

The disadvantage of zero-based budgeting is that it requires a large staff and increased time to prepare the budget. And it cannot be used in production or volume-sensitive areas.

Capital evaluation

When management is considering undertaking major capital projects, it must make a careful analysis of the costs and the anticipated return. This is especially critical when it is looking at a number of projects and the total costs far exceed the available capital. Since the company will say yes to some projects and no to others, it must have the best possible information in order to make the choice. Obviously, all of the costs and anticipated profits connected with each proposed project must be carefully identified.

Three techniques are commonly used to evaluate a capital spending project. While any one of the three can be employed, it's preferable to use all three together. They are:

- The pay-back method.
- Return on investment (ROI).
- Discounted cash flow (DCF).

The pay-back method

This relatively simple capital evaluation technique examines the time it will take for the project to earn back its cost--that is, how long the project must be in operation before the additional profits it generates equal the project cost.

For example, suppose a project has the following estimated costs and results:

Construction cost	$92,500
Debugging and start-up costs	7,500
Profit per year	30,000

In this case the pay-back period for the project is 3.33 years, which is calculated by dividing the total cost ($100,000) by the $30,000 annual profit.

Another factor probably should be added, although many analysts don't bother with it: the interest cost of the money borrowed to finance the project.

Alternatively, if the company had ample cash and did not have to borrow, the "opportunity cost" should be included; that is, the interest that could have be earned if the money had been invested rather than used to finance this project.

Return on investment method (ROI)

The project described above has a 30 percent return on investment (ROI), which simply means that the $30,000 profit expected each year is 30 percent of the project cost.

An alternative method of calculating ROI uses the average cost, taking depreciation into account, rather than the total cost. Suppose the project has an estimated useful life of 10 years and would be depreciated at the rate of $10,000 per year. The cost basis would be $100,000 at the beginning, $90,000 at the end of the first year, $80,000 at the end of the second year, and so on. The average cost over the 10-year period would be $50,000. Thus the average return on investment would be 60 percent ($30,000 divided by $50,000).

The ROI calculation leaves something to be desired if expected profits vary widely from one year to another. For example, it is common for smaller profits to be projected in the earlier years. Perhaps it takes time for the new product to catch on and for the plant to operate at capacity. The project might earn nothing in the first two years, $20,000 in the third year, and $40,000 a year after that.

The later profits are worth less to the company than if they were earned in the first year.* But a simple ROI calculation does not take that into account.

Discounted cash flow method (DCF)

This method does take into account the greater value of money now as opposed to money later. The formula determines the present value of money to be received in the future, based on the time interval until the money is received and the interest that is lost during that interval. The result, for any given time interval, will vary according to what interest rate is assumed and how often it is assumed to be compounded.

To illustrate, the following table shows the present value of money expected to be received over a ten-year period:

$1.00 to be received at the end of	Present value, assuming 10% interest compounded annually
Year 0	$1.00
1	.909
2	.826
3	.751
4	.683
5	.621
6	.564
7	.513
8	.466
9	.424
10	.386

Suppose that management has decided that capital projects should provide at least a 10 percent return; that means that the present value of all expected future profits will total at least 110 percent of the

---

*Money now is worth more than money later, because money now can be invested to earn more money. And money later is less desirable because its buying power is likely to be less because of inflation.

project's cost. And suppose that the discounted cash flow analysis of a $200,000 project looks like this:

Year	Cash flow	Present value
0	($200,000)	($200,000)
1	10,000	9,091
2	10,000	8,264
3	20,000	15,260
4	20,000	13,666
5	20,000	12,418
6 to 10	40,000/yr.	94,152*
Total	$ 80,000	($ 57,155)

*Sum of years 6 to 10

Clearly this project should not go forward. Not only does it fail to return 10 percent, but it actually produces a negative return.

Management decision-making

The budgeting and capital evaluation procedures we have discussed are immensely valuable in the management decision process, and sometimes they produce results that are unexpected.

For example, suppose a company has a single product and is considering whether to launch a second product. It determines that the research, development, tooling, and startup costs will be minimal. It also finds that the new product will require a minimum amount of management time and attention and can be sold by the present sales force. Moreover, it can be manufactured in the present plant on equipment already in place.

Thus there will be only a very modest addition to fixed costs. The product will have to carry its own variable costs, of course, but it may be a good business risk even though the new product will not contribute any-

114

thing to overhead. To put it another way, even though the new product may have a lower gross profit margin than the existing product, the decision to launch it may be a good one because it produces incremental profit, since the fixed cost burden is not significantly increased.

Similarly, a company may face a choice between buying a particular component from outside suppliers or tooling up to manufacture it in-house. In making this choice, it would prepare a detailed planning budget showing the estimated costs of production in house at various levels of volume. Presumably this cost would be less than the cost of purchase, but the question is whether the difference is great enough to justify the capital outlay. Thus, the next step is to make a discounted cash flow analysis of the capital expenditure, using the amount saved each year by in-house production as the "profit" earned on the investment.

Lease vs. purchase decision

Another very common management decision is the choice between buying a piece of equipment and leasing it. Suppose management is considering acquiring a machine with these financial characteristics:

Purchase cost:	$100,000
Useful life:	5 years
Salvage value:	$10,000
Depreciation method:	Sum of the years' digits

As an alternative to purchase, the machine can be leased at $2,000 per month for the same five years.

The purchase would require a large immediate outlay of cash (which might, of course, be borrowed) and a tax saving through the deduction of

115

noncash depreciation charges. Let us assume the company has a tax rate of 30 percent.

Lease payments will be made periodically in the future, and thus the DCF approach can be used to calculate the present cost of the future payments. This is the same formula that would be used to determine the present value of future income.

The choice involves a comparison between two DCF analyses. One is the present value of the cash saved by avoiding rental payments, calculated as a return on the capital expenditure of machine purchase. The other is the discounted present cost of future rental payments. Here are the figures at various assumed interest rates:

	Purchase	Lease
6%	$(49,200)	$(52,100)
8	(51,700)	(49,800)
10	(54,000)	(47,800)
12	(56,200)	(45,900)

Leasing looks more attractive at 8 percent or higher, while the purchase option looks better at 6 percent, If the figures are plotted on a graph, it will become apparent that the break-even point is at about 7.2 percent.

Chapter Eleven

ACCOUNTING ADJUSTMENTS FOR INFLATION

Inflation has presented the accounting system with a major problem; in fact, a whole set of problems. Inflation can cause financial statements prepared on the traditional historical cost basis to give very misleading impressions of a company's financial condition and operating results.

In this chapter we will see how inflation affects financial statements, and we will examine a number of ways of adjusting the figures for inflation. And we will see that the accounting profession has not yet reached any decision as to which adjustments should be required. It is still wrestling with the problem.

Understated asset values

One way that inflation distorts financial data is that the values stated on the balance sheet of assets, especially older assets, are seriously understated, as a result of inflation, in relation to current fair value and replacement cost.

Suppose that a company built a factory in 1964 for a total cost of $300,000, consisting of $50,000 for the land and $250,000 to construct the building. The land cannot be depreciated, but the building has now been written down through depreciation to $125,000. Thus the current book value is $175,000.

But the property could be sold today for $700,000. And the replacement cost might be considerably more. If the plant were destroyed by fire and had to be rebuilt, or if the company wanted to build a new plant of similar size in another location, the cost might well be $1,000,000 or more.

In a period of continuing inflation, asset values can be considerably understated in terms of both fair market or resale value and of replacement value. It is true that balance sheets should be conservative and that understatement is preferred to overstatement. But in many cases the understatement is so great as to give a false impression of the company's financial condition as a continuing business that has to renew and replace assets, and perhaps add to them, on a regular basis.

A company might have total capital assets (plant and equipment) with an original cost of $1,500,000 and a current book value of $900,000. If it wanted to increase its production capacity by 20 percent, it might find that a 20 percent increase in capital equipment would cost $1,500,000, or just as much as the original cost of all the capital equipment it now has.

Overstated profits

Other noncash assets are understated on the balance sheet, too. The understatement of inventory in relation to replacement cost can produce a very misleading impression of profits.

Let us consider a retail store that regularly sells large quantities of a particular nonperishable item at a 50 percent markup from its cost. It always has a supply of this item in inventory, and some of the stock on hand is now several years old. The books show inventory of this item purchased at these prices:

$$1977 \quad - \quad \$5.00$$
$$1978 \quad - \quad 5.45$$
$$1979 \quad - \quad 6.00$$
$$1980 \quad - \quad 6.60$$

The current selling price for this item is $9.90, representing a 50 percent markup from the $6.60 current cost. This produces a gross profit, before operating expenses and taxes, of $3.30 for each unit purchased in 1980. But for units purchased in 1977 the profit is $4.90, or almost 50 percent higher. The extra $1.60 is commonly referred to as inventory profit.

In an inflationary period, profits may be substantially overstated because a sizable part of the earnings represents inventory profit rather than real earnings. The overstatement is greatest for those companies that do not have a rapid inventory turnover.

Replacement cost accounting

The accounting profession has developed the replacement cost accounting method to adjust asset values that are understated because of inflation. This method does not produce a complete set of financial statements. Rather, it develops certain adjusted figures that can be used in the discretion of management and of analysts to provide a more meaningful picture of assets and profits.

Replacement cost accounting restates the value of capital assets, depreciation, and inventory to reflect current replacement costs. Here is an example of a set of replacement cost figures (note that they do not make up a complete statement):

	Historical cost	Replacement cost
Inventories	$ 98,767	$104,858
Plant and equipment	$459,609	$971,496
Less: accumulated depreciation	207,651	522,698
Net plant and equipment	$251,958	$448,798
Cost of sales	$701,139	$730,093
Current year's depreciation	$ 21,427	$ 40,921

Note that both the original cost and the depreciation reserve are adjusted to reflect the substantially higher replacement cost. The result is that the replacement value of the capital assets, adjusted for depreciation, is about $197,000 higher than current book value based on original depreciation cost. And the replacement value of inventories is about $6,000 higher than book value. Adding the two figures together, net worth is about $203,000 higher based on replacement, not book values.

However, profits are lower because cost of sales is higher by about $29,000, consisting of $19,000 in additional depreciation and about $10,000 in additional cost of inventory used in the current year's sales.

120

Thus the company's actual profit margin is considerably less, since its replacement cost investment is higher and its profits are lower.

The replacement value of assets is also important in connection with insurance coverage. Just as a homeowner should constantly increase his insurance coverage to reflect the growing value of the house, a business should have insurance covering the fair market value, or, if possible, the replacement value. The assets would be grossly underinsured if the coverage was based on original cost.

Tax assessments are also affected. Unfortunately for the company, the tax assessor will probably assess real estate and personal property taxes according to current value rather than original cost.

Price level or constant dollar accounting

This is another inflation-adjusting accounting method. Although somewhat more comprehensive than replacement cost accounting, it does not produce a complete set of financial statements.

The basic principle of price level or constant dollar accounting is to adjust all historical figures to the current value of the dollar. Since today's dollar is worth less than at any time in the past, all previously stated figures will be adjusted upward. It has been determined that the adjustments will be based on the Consumer Price Index for All Urban Consumers (CPI-U),* which is calculated and published every month by the Bureau

---

*This determination was made by the Financial Accounting Standards Board, the standard-setting body of the accounting profession, in its statement No. 33, "Financial Reporting and Changing Prices." Questions have been raised about the appropriateness of using the CPI-U index, and some analysts believe that it diverges sharply from business indexes, perhaps because of the weight it gives to steadily escalating costs of residential housing. Thus it is possible that a different index may be chosen in the future.

of Labor Statistics of the U.S. Department of Labor.

The CPI-U index uses 1967 as a base year. Here are the CPI-U figures for a number of recent years:

1967	100.00
1970	116.3
1975	161.2
1977	181.5
1978	195.3
1979	219.4

The CPI-U index figures are used to develop adjustment factors for each year in question. For example, the 1977 adjustment factor is determined this way:

$$\frac{1979 \text{ CPI-U Index}}{1977 \text{ CPI-U Index}} = \frac{219.4}{181.5} = 1.209$$

The adjustment factors for the years shown are:

1967	2.194
1970	1.887
1975	1.361
1977	1.209
1978	1.123
1979	1.000

These figures tell us that it took $1.887 in 1979 dollars to buy what cost $1.00 in 1970. Or, looked at another way, if the company had cash on hand of $100,000 in 1970, that is the equivalent of having $188,700 on hand at the end of 1979.

It is readily apparent that a new set of adjustment factors will be developed for 1980. The 1979 adjustment factor will be greater than 1.000 and all the others will be increased, too.

122

The adjustment factors can be applied as desired to fixed assets, inventories, or any other assets on balance sheets compiled in the past. The adjusted asset value will always be higher than historical cost, unless we enter a deflationary period in which the CPI-U declines.

Here is a simplified example of the application of constant dollar adjustments to the valuation of fixed assets. It is assumed that a company regularly acquires capital assets with an estimated useful life of 20 years, and straight line depreciation is used:

Year of acquisition	Historical cost	Cost	Depreciated (20-year life)	% Accumulated depreciation
1979	$10,000	$10,000	5	$ 500
1978	10,000	11,230	10	1,123
1977	10,000	12,090	15	1,623
1975	10,000	13,610	25	3,402
1970	10,000	18,870	45	8,491
Totals	$50,000	$78,800		$15,139

Accumulated depreciation	$10,500	$15,139
Net P.P. & E.	$39,500	$63,661

The difference between $39,500, the depreciated historical cost basis, and $63,661, the depreciated constant-dollar adjusted cost basis, is the inflation component. It is the increase in the plant account as a result of inflation.

Constant dollar adjustment of asset values always increases them in an inflationary period. By contrast, the adjustment of liabilities on past balance sheets will reduce them. As the value of the dollar declines, debt is repaid in cheaper dollars. Or, if constant dollar adjustment is used to make all dollars equal, then it takes fewer dollars this year to repay debts incurred in past years:

Year ending December 31	Debt	Average CPI-U for year	Adjustment factor	Current value in constant $
1979	$100,000	219.4	1.000	$100,000
1978	100,000	195.3	1.123	112,300
1977	100,000	181.5	1.209	120,900
1975	100,000	161.2	1.361	136,100
1970	100,000	116.3	1.887	188,700

While it would be possible to prepare a full balance sheet on a constant dollar adjusted basis, most companies do not do this and it has not yet been established as a requirement by the Financial Accounting Standards Board. This is due in part to the difficulties involved in evaluating mineral lands and some buildings that, on a constant dollar basis, would have values with no relationship to changes in the price level.

A typical partial report using constant dollars would be:

	Historical cost	Adjusted for inflation
Net sales	$863,000	$863,000
Cost of sales	788,000	809,000 (A)
Net income	$ 75,000	$ 54,000
Income taxes	30,000	30,000 (B)
Net income	$ 45,000	$ 24,000
Shareholders' equity	$305,000	459,000 (C)
Gain from decline in purchasing power of net amounts owed		$ 17,000 (D)

(A) The increase results from higher depreciation allowances on revalued assets and from higher cost of acquiring inventory.

(B) The tax laws do not permit adjustment for inflation, thus income taxes do not change.

(C) The substantial increase in net worth results from a sizable increase in the value of capital assets through constant dollar adjustment.

(D) This gain results from the payment of debts with cheaper dollars, or with a smaller number of constant dollars.

Current cost accounting

This is another method of adjusting financial statements for changing price levels and the declining value of the dollar. It is similar to replacement cost accounting but applies to all the assets on the balance sheet, while replacement cost accounting is used only for inventory and certain fixed assets.

Unlike constant dollar accounting, which applies the same adjustment factor to all the figures for a particular year, current cost accounting makes a separate adjustment for each item. Some adjustments are much larger than others.

Here is an example of current cost accounting:

Product Y
Historical Cost vs. Current Cost
December 31, 1980

	Historical cost	Current cost
Cost of machine	$100,000	$350,000
Useful life	20 years	20 years
Annual depreciation	5,000	17,500
Insurance costs	500	1,750
Interest costs	2,000	10,000
Taxes	300	1,250
Total	$ 7,800	$ 30,500
Annual production	10,000 units	10,000 units
Capital associated costs/unit	.78	3.05
All other costs	3.00	3.50
Total costs	$3.78	$6.55
Selling price	$5.00	$5.00
Profit (loss)/unit	$1.22	($1.55)
Profit margin	24.4%	Negative

This analysis takes into account not only the increase in the current cost of the machine but also increases in insurance, interest, taxes, and other costs connected with the production of the item. And it makes clear that what appeared, based on historical cost figures, to be a profitable product is in fact an unprofitable one.

Current cost accounting and other methods of adjusting for inflation almost always have the effect of increasing the stated value of assets and of reducing profits. However, occasionally there is an exception. In industries such as electronics that have experienced very rapid technological advances, the cost of acquiring equipment and inventory may actually decline, even in an inflationary period. In other words, technology is reducing costs even faster than inflation is increasing them. Thus a few companies may show higher rather than lower profits when the income account is adjusted by current cost accounting.

The problem—which adjustments to use?

The accounting profession and its regulatory bodies are now wrestling with the problems of inflation adjustments but have not reached any final conclusion. It is clear that the traditional historical cost approach can produce figures that are very misleading. But inflation-adjusted figures can be misleading, too.

Most accounting professionals agree that historical cost figures should not be abandoned and completely replaced by inflation-adjusted figures. But there seems to be a consensus that inflation-adjusted figures are valuable, perhaps even essential. The profession seems to be moving in the direction of using inflation-adjusted figures as a supplement to historical cost figures. That is, two sets of statements would be issued so that management and analysts can use either or both.

The Securities and Exchange Commission is already requiring publicly owned companies to supplement their published financial statements with replacement cost data covering certain assets and, beginning with 1979 annual reports, with current cost accounting adjustments of many of the key figures. For example, General Motors reported net income for 1979 of $2.8 billion on the historical cost basis but only $1.8 billion with constant dollar adjustment.

Beginning with 1980 statements, all audited financial statements will be required to present constant dollar adjusted figures. And publicly owned companies will present current cost adjustments as well.

Chapter Twelve

YOU AND YOUR ACCOUNTANT

The company's outside accounting firm is usually more involved in the company's day-to-day operations and knows more about them than almost anyone except senior management. Unlike the company's outside lawyers, for example, who are generally called upon only when a specific problem needs to be dealt with, the accountants are involved with the company's business and finances on a continuing basis.

Moreover, they have access to internal financial data, such as breakdowns of revenue, expenses, and profits, that are closely guarded by top management. Frequently the outside accountants are privy to information that is not even given to the board of directors.

The accountants are almost always involved whenever financial information is supplied to anyone outside the company. If the company borrows from a bank, the bankers will rely heavily upon financial statements that are either prepared by or confirmed by the outside accountants. Similarly,

128

suppliers who extend credit will normally ask to see financial information and will rely upon it in determining how much credit to make available to the company.

If the company is publicly owned, the accountants will have a central role in the preparation and certification of financial statements that are filed with the Securities and Exchange Commission and sent to stockholders, and that also become a matter of public record. Thus they are available for scrutiny by newspaper reporters and the general public.

Financial statements published annually at the end of the company's fiscal year must be certified by the company's outside accountants. Interim statements, which are generally briefer and less detailed, are usually published quarterly, although sometimes monthly or semiannually. They are not certified but are reviewed by the accountants for reasonableness.

Auditing the company's books

The most important function of the outside accountants is to examine or audit the company's books and financial records and to certify the company's financial statements. The special value and importance of the certification arises from the fact that it is provided by skilled professionals who are independent and who are not under the control of management or obligated to management in any way.

The audit does not guarantee the absolute accuracy of every single entry in the company's books. This would be virtually impossible, since the only way the outside accountants could provide such a high degree of assurance would be to review every entry and every transaction. In effect, it would have to do all of the company's bookkeeping over again, and that would be prohibitively expensive.

Rather than review and repeat the bookkeeping entries for each transaction, the auditors* test or spot-check a sample consisting of a number of transactions of each type. The size of the sample is determined statistically according to the total number of transactions and the size and importance of transactions of that particular type. By this sampling technique, the auditors can estimate the reliability of the total number of transactions to a 95 percent to 99 percent degree of accuracy.

The audit consists of four basic functions:

• Review of internal controls.

• Review of bookkeeping procedures and maintenance of the books.

• Verification of assets and liabilities.

• Preparation of the report.

Review of internal controls

An essential part of the audit function is to examine and review the internal controls by which the company keeps track of assets--not only cash but other assets, too. The controls should prevent fraud and embezzlement, as well as less sinister losses such as waste caused by sloppy record-keeping and ordinary carelessness.

For example, the auditors will interview warehouse clerks and others who have the authority to release items from inventory, and they will exam-

*In the business world it is common to use the words auditors and accountants interchangeably. Strictly speaking, anybody can be an auditor and examine books, even a five-year-old child. But in common parlance, and in this chapter, the words audit and auditors refer to outside accountants who are examining the company's books, unless the context indicates otherwise.

130

ine the inventory procedures and controls. They must satisfy themselves that the controls are tight, that systematic procedures are in place and are being followed, and that it is difficult or impossible for inventory to be removed without being properly authorized and accounted for. This examination applies to finished goods, components, and raw materials, and also to such items as vehicles, tools and equipment, and packing boxes and supplies.

The control of cash is crucial, of course, and the auditors thoroughly examine all procedures and systems for handling cash and checks, both incoming and outgoing. And they examine the controls and procedures for preparation and approval of invoices to customers and payments to suppliers and others. For example, the auditors will inquire whether the person who approves the payment of invoices also has the authority to sign checks. This is considered a dangerous practice, and they would almost certainly recommend that it be changed.

At the time they submit their report they may recommend other changes in internal procedures and controls that may be desirable. In rare cases they might find the controls so loose and deficient that they would be unable to express an opinion as to the accuracy of the financial statements.

Review of maintenance of the books

The auditors will review carefully a statistically determined number of transactions to ensure that they have been recorded properly and accurately. In the course of this review of individual transactions, they also examine the company's bookkeeping routine and procedures, to determine whether the books are kept in an orderly manner and whether the bookkeeping sequence (pages 21-28) is being followed properly.

Verification of assets and liabilities

The auditors take steps to verify that the assets and liabilities shown on the balance sheet actually exist in the amounts shown. They will verify all cash items by sending letters to banks, other depositories, and brokers asking for written confirmation of the company's account balance as of the statement date. Certificates of government securities or other bonds or stocks will be examined. Principal fixed assets, such as factory buildings and warehouses, will be inspected.

Other assets and liabilities will undergo a sample verification. For example, the auditors will review the accounts receivable and send letters to a number of customers (but not all) asking for written confirmation that the customer owes the amount shown on the company's books. Accounts payable will also be sample verified by sending letters to suppliers and to other creditors.

Preparation of the report

When the auditors have completed their review and examination, they prepare a set of financial statements--a balance sheet, an income statement, and a flow of funds statement. In theory, these statements are prepared by management and merely certified by the auditors. But in practice, especially in smaller companies that may lack sophistication in financial management, the auditors play a major part in the actual preparation of the statements. For example, they may advise management that the recording of a particular transaction appears to be improper and they may "suggest" that it be handled in a different way. Their suggestion is not likely to be ignored, since they might withhold their certification of financial statements that they considered to include improper entries.

The auditors' certificate

The end product of the auditors' work--and perhaps their most important function--is their opinion letter or certificate attesting to the accuracy and completeness of the company's financial statements. Here is an example of such a certificate:

REPORT OF INDEPENDENT CERTIFIED PUBLIC ACCOUNTANTS

To the Board of Directors and Shareholders of XYZ Company, Incorporated:

We have examined the balance sheets of the XYZ Company, as of December 21, 1980 and 1979, and the related statements of income, shareholders' equity, and changes in financial position for the years then ended, and the related supporting schedules. Our examination was made in accordance with generally accepted auditing standards and, accordingly, included such tests of the accounting records and such other auditing procedures as we considered necessary in the circumstances.

In our opinion, the financial statements referred to above present fairly the financial position of the XYZ Company at December 31, 1980 and 1979, and the results of their operations and changes in their financial position for the years then ended, and the related supporting schedules present fairly the information to be included therein, all in conformity with generally accepted accounting principles applied on a consistent basis.

A.B. & C.
(signature)
Certified Public Accountants

What the certificate says

This relatively brief certification letter is very important to the company, its owners, and its creditors, and it is essential to understand why certain words and phrases are used and exactly what they mean.

Here are the key elements of the accountants' letter:

1. The CPAs are independent. Although they are retained and paid by the company, they have arrived at their conclusions without pressure or influence from company management.

2. The certificate applies only to those financial statements that are identified in the first sentence, not to any other statements. The statements and the certificate may be included in an annual report, but other tables, charts, and statistics that may be prepared by management for inclusion in the annual report are not covered by the certificate.

3. The audit and the certificate cover only the statements for the two years 1980 and 1979.

4. The accountants followed generally accepted auditing standards (page 136).

5. The audit involved a test of accounting records, not a complete review of every single transaction of the company during the two years.

6. The figures are presented in accordance with generally accepted accounting principles, which have been uniformly applied during the period, except as otherwise indicated in the certificate or in the notes to the financial statements. (For example, if there had been a change between 1979 and 1980 in depreciation methods or from FIFO to LIFO, that would be noted.) Generally accepted accounting principles are followed throughout the world and apply to all audited statements. They are established in this country by the Financial Accounting Standards Board (FASB).

7. The accountants' signature is important because it means that

creditors and others may rely on the validity of the figures presented. If it were to turn out later that the auditors had been negligent or had failed to follow generally accepted auditing standards or accounting principles, anyone who relied upon the figures might have a claim for damages against the accounting firm.

Exceptions in the certificate

The certificate set forth on page 133 is what businessmen refer to as a "clean" certificate. That is, the financial statements that the accountants examined are found to be in order. Sometimes, however, they find it necessary to express a reservation in the certificate.

Here is an example. Suppose the company is a manufacturer of auto parts, and that Chrysler is its largest customer, accounting for over half of its sales. Suppose further that it had a substantial investment in tools and dies used to produce parts for shipment to Chrysler, and that it had substantial accounts receivable from Chrysler. In this situation, the accountants would probably be willing to give an opinion letter but they would express a reservation that the demise of Chrysler, if it occurred, might have a seriously detrimental effect upon the company and its net worth, and indeed might even endanger its survival.

An exception or reservation in the certificate is an extremely serious matter for a publicly owned company; it usually has a damaging effect upon the price of its stock. What would be much more serious, though, would be a refusal by the accountants to give any certificate at all. This occasionally happens, either because of a serious dispute between the accountants and the management, or because the company is in serious financial trouble, or both. The accountants' refusal to certify would constitute a company crisis of the first magnitude and would cause great anxiety among creditors and suppliers. In all probability, if the company were publicly owned the SEC would suspend trading of the stock.

Generally accepted auditing standards

In 1963, the American Institute of CPAs established certain basic auditing standards that all CPAs are expected to observe. (These standards relate to the conduct of the auditors and the procedures they follow, as distinguished from the accounting principles set forth by FASB.) These standards are:

1. General standards. The audit is to be performed by an accountant who is properly trained, technically qualified, and proficient as an auditor. All those involved in conducting the audit will exercise due professional care and--very important--will maintain an independent attitude of mind and will not alter their procedures or their conclusions because of pressure from management.

2. Field work standards. The work of the audit must be well planned, organized, and supervised. Original documents, such as mortgage notes, bank loan agreements, customer or supplier contracts, will be examined where necessary to support the auditors' opinion of the accuracy of the financial data associated with those transactions. Internal controls will be evaluated to determine how much reliance should be placed upon internally generated figures.

3. Standards of reporting. The report and the certification letter will follow the standards set forth on pages 132-133.

Other activities of outside accountants

In smaller companies, the outside accountants are often called upon to assist in setting up bookkeeping procedures and supervising the book-keeping operation. This is very common, especially if the company's management is not conversant with bookkeeping procedures. However, using the outside accountants for the actual bookkeeping is much too expensive; it would be better to hire an experienced part-time bookkeeper if there is not enough work to justify full-time help.

Outside accountants are sometimes called upon to make special financial studies of, for example, new products or a move into a new market. And they may be retained to make appraisals of a piece of property or of a company that is under consideration for acquisition.

Many companies use their outside accountants to prepare income and franchise tax returns.

In recent years, some accounting firms have expanded their services beyond the accounting area. They now have executive search departments and actuarial and pension plan services, and some also offer a variety of management consulting and financial consulting services. Among these are assistance in the design and installation of data processing systems and merger and acquisition studies.

Training and licensing of accountants

An accountant is required to have college-level training in accounting and related fields such as business law, finance, and statistics. Virtually all accountants have a bachelor's degree, though it is not an absolute requirement for employment in the field.

A working accountant is not necessarily a CPA (Certified Public Accountant). The CPA certificate is granted by the various states, after an extremely rigorous examination, usually lasting at least two full days. Virtually all states require a bachelor's degree and some work experience before the test is taken.

In most accounting firms, all of the accounting practice partners are CPAs, though this is not necessarily required. Many of the employees will also be CPAs, and generally the junior employees will be planning to take the CPA examination and accumulating the required experience.

Accountants' fees

Accountants charge on a time basis--so much per hour or per day. The charges can vary widely, according to the rank and experience level of the personnel working on a given job. In 1980 charges will rarely be less than $25-$30 per hour for even the most junior employees of the accounting firm, and they may go as high as $175 per hour, possibly even higher, for the firm's most experienced and most senior partners. A smaller company may rarely see a partner of the firm, which is probably just as well, since the nonpartner employees bill at much lower rates. In such a case, however, the employee generally works under the supervision of a partner who reviews and spot-checks his work and is available for consultation if problems arise.

Selecting an outside accountant

Choosing an accountant is very much like selecting any other professional adviser--a doctor, lawyer, architect, management consultant, or financial adviser. That is to say, it isn't easy. One can rarely discern in an initial interview how skillful and imaginative the accountant is, whether his charges will be reasonable, and whether a comfortable working relationship will develop. This is essential, because the accountant and management will be working closely together on highly confidential matters. Only by actually retaining the firm can the company learn whether they will be compatible.

Many companies choose their accountant on the basis of personal acquaintance or by asking friends in the management of other companies for recommendations. Some accounting firms specialize in a particular industry and can do a better job for the company by virtue of their expertise in that field.

It frequently happens that the first accounting firm chosen by a company will be a small local firm that can handle its work adequately and will probably charge less than a larger firm. Later, as the company grows, it may switch to a larger firm because it finds it needs a higher degree of experience and sophistication and a broader range of services than the smaller firm can provide. Moreover, especially if the company goes public, it may feel that it needs the name and reputation of one of the national firms to give its figures greater credibility with investors and with security analysts.

A small company that plans either to change outside accountants or to retain outside accountants for the first time would be well advised to interview two or three firms, encouraging them to compete for the company's work and asking them to explain what kind of a job they would do and to estimate their charges.

How to fire an accountant

Accountants don't have a contract--they are retained for as long as the company is satisfied with their work and they can be discharged whenever management so decides. If the accountants are to be dismissed, it should be done as smoothly and in as friendly a way as possible. The change should be explained in advance to creditors and lenders, who may be greatly alarmed if it comes as a surprise.

Some companies make a practice of changing accountants from time to time in order to get new perspectives and new ideas on financial management and internal controls.

Internal auditors

Some companies have an in-house audit group that performs the same functions as the outside accountants. That is, it reviews internal controls, spot-checks transactions, and verifies assets in order to prevent fraud. The internal audit group is normally kept separate from the other accounting and financial management personnel as a means of assuring its independence. Usually this group reports directly to and has its salaries established by the owner of the company or the chairman of the board, rather than the controller.

If the internal auditors do their job properly, the outside accountants will soon come to rely on their work to a considerable degree. As the outside accountants' workload diminishes, their charges are correspondingly reduced.

APPENDIX A

The ABC Company
Balance Sheet

December 31, 1979

Current assets
Cash $ 9,353
Marketing securities (U.S. Treasury Bills)   27,649
Accounts and notes receivable:
  Total $109,023
  Less: Allowance for doubtful accounts   8,713   100,310
Inventories   76,013
Prepaid expense   6,588
  Total $219,913

Current liabilities
Accounts payable $52,083
Current installment on long-term debt   11,128
Accrued expenses   35,172
  Total $ 98,383

Working capital $121,530

Plant, property and equipment $509,325
Less: Allowances for depreciation and depletion   224,289   285,036

Investments   24,864
Other assets   21,771
Funds employed in the business $453,201

Long-term debt   149,188
Deferred income taxes   35,635
Shareholders' equity $268,378

Shareholders' equity consisting of:
Preferred stock   2,727
Common stock   35,412
Capital surplus   58,962
Retained earnings   171,835
Treasury stocks   (558)

  Total $268,378

142

APPENDIX B

The ABC Company
Statement of Income
Year ending December 31, 1979

Net sales		$730,175
Less: Cost of goods sold		585,994
Gross profit		$144,181
Less: Selling, general and administrative expenses		67,594
Operating income		$ 76,587
Less: Interest expense	$13,055	
Plus: Other income	1,807	11,248
Profit before taxes		$ 65,339
Provision for income taxes		27,618
Net income		$ 37,721

APPENDIX C

XYZ Company
Flow of Funds Statement
Year ending December 31, 1979

Funds provided from:

Net income	$ 37,721
Items not affecting working capital:	
Depreciation and depletion	30,043
Deferred income taxes	2,671
Funds provided from operations	70,435
Increase in long-term debt	18,366
Disposal of property, plant and equipment	6,211
Total sources	95,012

Funds used for:

Additions to property, plant and equipment	47,955
Purchase of treasury stock	558
Reduction of long-term debt	12,392
Cash dividends paid	9,702
Total uses	70,607
Net increase in working capital	24,405

Changes in working capital:

Cash	35,506
Accounts receivable	7,659
Inventories	2,206
Accounts payable	(11,987)
Income taxes payable	(8,160)
Other	1,181
Net increase in working capital	24,405

XYZ Company
Cash Flow Statement
Month of December 1979

Cash balance: November 30, 1979

Sources of cash:		$ 38,000
Net sales	$162,000	
Less: Increase in Accounts receivable	12,000	150,000
Increase in notes payable		10,000
Sale of used machinery		20,000
Total cash available		218,000
Uses of cash:		
Purchase of goods and services	150,000	
Plus: Decrease in accounts payable	10,000	160,000
Payment of cash dividend		10,000
Purchase of new machine		10,000
Total uses		180,000
Cash balance: December 31, 1979		38,000

APPENDIX D

XYZ Company
Cash Flow Statement
Month of January, 1980

Sources of cash
Net sales	$100,000	
Less: Increase in Accounts receivable	5,000	$ 95,000
Sale of assets		5,000
Issuance of long-term debt		25,000
Issuance of common stock		5,000
Total sources		$130,000

Uses of Cash
Payroll		$ 50,000
Materials purchased	$ 40,000	
Plus: Decrease in accounts payable	5,000	45,000
Purchase of machine		25,000
Total uses of cash		$120,000
Net increase in cash		$ 10,000

Cash balance, January 31, 1980	$ 51,000
Cash balance, January 1, 1980	41,000
Net increase in cash	$ 10,000

INDEX

150